MURDER IN MARPLE

THE D'AMORE FAMILY TRAGEDY

MURDER IN MARPLE

THOMAS GEORGE DEITMAN
WITH DAWN D'AMORE YANKANICH

THE History PRESS

Published by The History Press
Charleston, SC 29403
www.historypress.net

All illustrations by Sally Klann.

First published 2015

Manufactured in the United States

ISBN 978.1.46711.794.4

Library of Congress Control Number: 2015946487

Notice: The information in this book is true and complete to the best of our knowledge. It is offered without guarantee on the part of the author or The History Press. The author and The History Press disclaim all liability in connection with the use of this book.

For
Olivia and Otis

CONTENTS

PREFACE

In the late summer of 1989, two brothers, Lyle and Erik Menendez, murdered their father and mother, Jose and Kitty, as the couple relaxed in the family room of their home in Beverly Hills, California. The brothers' weapon of choice was a Mossberg twelve-gauge shotgun. The father was shot, point blank, in the back of the head, and the mother's face was blown away by the blast of the powerful weapon.

The case drew worldwide attention. Both the print and the electronic media inundated the public with every minute detail of the crime and the events that led up to it. Their motive, both boys claimed, was their need to rid themselves of an abusive father and a mentally unstable mother.

The brothers, who lived the good life in Southern California, said that they lived in fear of their parents, that they had been victims of both sexual and physical abuse at the hands of their father and that their mother, addled by drugs and drinking, allowed the mistreatment to go on and, in some cases, took part in it.

In the end, the defense of fear did not hold up. The jury concluded that the real motive was greed. Jose Menendez was a wealthy man, and the brothers weren't satisfied waiting for a small piece of the action—they wanted it right then, and they wanted it all. The Menendez brothers sealed their legal fate by partying it up after the murder. The real motive behind the murder was made pretty clear to the jury by the actions of the boys themselves.

In November 1949, Marple Township, Pennsylvania, was about as far away from 1989 Beverly Hills as anyone could get. Even today, Marple, located in suburban Philadelphia, Delaware County, is a far cry from the glitz, glitter, glamour and wealth of Southern California. That's not to say the Marple Township is not a good place to live. The homes are well kept, and the citizens are active in the community. It is a typical middle- to upper-middle-class suburb. However, Marple does have one thing in common with Beverly Hills: murder.

Forty years before the Menendez brothers executed their father and mother, a crime of chilling similarity took place in quiet Marple Township. It was a homicide committed by two brothers with their father as the target. One of the weapons used was a shotgun. The motive, according to the brothers, was an abusive family life. However, to this day, some believe that money was the real reason the two sons murdered their father.

At the time, the crime was big news in Delaware County, and the local paper, the *Chester Times* (now the *Delaware County Daily Times*), covered the case extensively. Even the Philadelphia dailies got in on the act. But in 1948, there was no Internet, no Court TV and no MSNBC, so after the trial, the news coverage ended, and the murder of a father by his two sons slipped into historical oblivion—until now.

ACKNOWLEDGEMENTS

When I first started this project, I thought, "This should be easy—just research some facts, figure out a logical order and go ahead and write the stuff." Boy was I wrong! What I did not take into account was the fact that the D'Amore murder took place in 1949, and while it was big news back then, very few people alive today even know about it. Actually, people know of it rather than about it. There are not a whole lot of first-person witness accounts, written documents or people left alive who had anything to do with the actual incident.

As I said before, most, if not all, of the facts surrounding the murder and the subsequent trial come from newspaper articles written in 1949 and 1950. The fact is that it took help from people to look at those articles, analyze them and juxtapose them with today's events in order to get a better picture of how things were handled and perceived in 1949 and 1950. These people deserve a great deal of thanks for their help.

It goes without saying that Dawn D'Amore Yankanich deserves the most thanks. Dawn took a chance in order to have this story told. Not many of us are willing to open ourselves and our families to scrutiny as Dawn has done. Usually, when a family carries a past tragedy, they want to keep it within the group, but Dawn wanted just the opposite. She wanted people to know that a murder took place; she wanted people to know that her grandfather was a cruel and abusive individual; she wanted people to know that her two uncles, Nicholas and John, had no other recourse to save the family from future abuse than by doing away with the one person who created that horrible environment: their father, Benjamin D'Amore. She also wanted to know if there was any other reason the two boys did what they did. Was it greed or revenge that drove them to murder their father? She needed to know the answers because the truth would allow her to clear her mind of the terrible secret, and in doing so, she would finally be able to understand how the events of that November night in 1949 impacted her family then and even now. Dawn exhibited a great amount of courage by allowing her thoughts and life to be left bare.

I also owe her husband a debt of gratitude. He supported both his wife and my project without question. He also showed a great deal of courage in doing so.

To the others who contributed, I give my sincere gratitude:

Thanks to retired Philadelphia Police Department detective Mike Fahy, who examined the 1949 case from a 2015 point of view and, in doing so, was able to provide insight on how present-day investigative methods and modern crime scene investigation techniques might have been used to expand the handling of the murder scene.

Thanks to Matthew C. Stone, esquire. Matt is a practicing attorney in Delaware County. He did much the same thing with the trial as Mike Fahy did with the crime scene. Matt looked at some of the more unusual aspects of the trial from today's legal mindset and was very helpful in translating these events into modern judicial procedures. Suffice it to say that some of what happened during the trial seems, to today's legal minds, to be downright humorous and beyond any concept of modern-day courtroom procedure.

Thanks to Dr. Shana Maier, associate professor and director of the master of arts in criminal justice program at Widener University in Chester, Pennsylvania. Dr. Maier's knowledge of spousal abuse, the intergenerational cycle of violence and the status of abused woman in the late 1940s was so very insightful when it came to understanding the issues that troubled the D'Amore family.

Thanks to Phil Heron, currant editor of the *Delaware County Daily Times*, the next generation print child of the old *Chester Times*. Phil graciously allowed me the permission to make use of quotes from various editions of the *Chester Times*, as that paper covered the story of the murder and the trial.

Thanks to Katie Orlando of The History Press. Katie guided me through the workings of book publishing and the hows of the 2015 computer world (especially DropBox). Katie also deserves so much credit for her patience, since I missed almost every deadline that The History Press assigned to me.

Thanks also to Candice Lawrence, also of The History Press. Candice took over as my guide through the final stages of the publishing process when Katie Orlando left to return to college.

ACKNOWLEDGEMENTS

Thanks to Susan E. Truesdale, first deputy clerk of courts for Delaware County. Susan took time from her busy schedule to talk with me about the trial and to give me some helpful ideas on where to find additional information.

Thanks to Rich Paul, chair of the Marple Township Historical Committee. Rich was instrumental in connecting me to Jack Smith and Ted Muahlmatt.

Thanks to Jack Smith and Ted Muehlmatt, both longtime Marple Township residents and schoolmates of the D'Amore children, for meeting with me and passing along their remembrances of the D'Amore family and the public's reaction to the verdict.

Of course, there are others who helped in numerous ways, including the staff of the mapping section of Delaware County and the staff of Sts. Peter and Paul Cemetery, which helped me locate the D'Amore family graves and also taught me how to move around the cemetery using the location code for each plot (not as easy as you might think!).

Thank you to Marge Johnson—coordinator of the Delaware County Historical Society—along with all the society volunteers, for guidance during my historical research. Marge and her group put in hour after hour archiving the varied histories of Delaware County and the communities that exist within the county borders.

Sally Klann did the wonderful illustrations that grace the pages of this work. Sally is a painter and an illustrator and lives in Ocean Beach in San Diego, California. I first became familiar with Sally's work while reading another true crime book, and the drawings that accompanied that work jumped off the pages at me. I asked Sally if she would illustrate my book, and she agreed, much to my delight. Sally is originally from Fairfield, Connecticut, and holds a bachelor's degree in art from Whitman College in Walla Walla, Washington. It is an honor for me to have Sally's work highlight my words. Please check out Sally's other artwork at her website, www.sallyklann.com.

Finally, thanks to two others in my life. Thank you to my wife, Olivia, the only self-actualized person that I have ever met. Olivia just kept telling me to put on my writer's hat even when I felt that I had permanently misplaced it. (She has a mental hat for everything that I am supposed to do, a clean-up-around-the house hat, a clean-up-the-back-yard hat, et cetera.) And thank you to Otis, our late and great Boston terrier, who hung out under the desk as I was writing and who, exercising on the patience that only dogs seem to have, listened, without protest, as I read what I was writing.

INTRODUCTION

I had been researching some material for a book that I was writing, outlining the evolution of crime, law enforcement and the judicial system in southeastern Pennsylvania from the 1600s, so I posted a note on local social media, hoping that I could find some additional material. Instead, I received a reply from a woman named Dawn D'Amore Yankanich, who wondered if I would be interested in meeting with her and allowing her to tell me her story. She said that it had to do with her two uncles and how they murdered her grandfather Benjamin D'Amore.

To say the least, a story like that was worth a cup of coffee. I met with Dawn, and she outlined the entire incident. She brought along a very personal piece that she had written about her childhood and the crime. She also brought numerous original newspaper articles that had been published from the time of the crime until the verdict was announced.

Dawn said she thought it was time to tell the story in detail since the two brothers were dead, and her father, a third brother, had recently passed away. It didn't take me much time to say yes and that I would be happy to write the story of the crime and how it has affected Dawn and her family.

As normally happens when somebody starts digging into the background of people or investigates the facts of an event, interesting and sometimes strange things start to appear. It is not unusual that these happenings and people lead the investigator down roads that he or she never thought existed. In life, nothing is ever what it seems. There is always the A-side and the C-side yet the real story always falls somewhere in the middle—on the B-side, so to speak.

That is what exactly happened once I started to delve into the facts about the D'Amore family, the murder and the trial. Of course, the murder took place in 1949, and the trial started at the beginning of 1950, so there were some things I found that could be chalked up to the attitude of the times. However, it's fair to say that when it comes to legal issues, whether the decade is the 1950s or the 2010s, some things should be the same. After all, the American system of jurisprudence is based on the adversary system, and the prosecution and defense lawyers still argue the cases and battle over whom to select as members of the jury panel. The judges still preside in an unbiased manner toward the individuals involved.

In the *Commonwealth v. D'Amore* trial, this was not always the case. To me, the prosecutor made several questionable judgments when it came to trial tactics and *voir dire*, the period in a trial when both the defense and the prosecuting attorneys get to directly question members of the prospective jury pool. The trial judge made some interesting rulings in favor of the defense, and at the end of the trial after the verdict was read, he allowed the defense attorney to thank the jury in a rather unusual way. His public admonishment to the two defendants, after the verdict was read, showed a clear misunderstanding of the importance and severity of the case.

The police agency, in whose jurisdiction the crime was committed, seemed to overlook some important information and may have rushed to a conclusion without a more intense investigation. Of course, it was 1949, and the police did not have the wherewithal to employ the scientific CSI procedures that they would have used had the murder been committed in 2015.

According to the defendants, they murdered their father in order to end a relationship ripe with mental and physical abuse laid on all members of the family. The question arises: how could abuse rise to the level of severity that it ended in murder? Well, it was an era when women were treated differently. Spousal and child abuse was not considered an important crime and, for the most part, was left to the families to work out. The cops had better things to do with their time and more important crimes to investigate. It was also a time when everybody know everybody else, and friendship often trumped the fact that someone committed a crime and should have been called to task for his or her actions.

Another interesting lesson about abuse is that it can carry on, down from one generation to another. Children who were abused can become abusers themselves, even performing the same abusive acts on their wives and children that were performed on them.

And, of course, when it comes to most murders, there always seems to be a back story of supposition, opinion and conclusions based on what people think is the real reason for the crime. The D'Amore case is no different. Abuse may not have been the real reason that the brothers killed their father; rather, greed may have made them pull the triggers. But since the family was abused by the father, abuse seemed like the logical explanation.

Because of the lack of records and because most of the people involved in the shooting are long dead, the real motive for the D'Amore boys executing their father may never be known. What is known is that they did commit the crime, and taking all the facts into consideration, it does make for an unusual and interesting story.

One important issue that I would like to address has to do with the coverage of the trial itself. After talking to individuals at the Delaware County Courthouse in Media, I could find no official court transcripts of the trial proceedings. Interestingly, Delaware County maintains very thorough archival records of indictments, true bills and transcripts in the county archives library in a location about three miles from the courthouse itself. At this point, however, these records cover only a period of time between 1789 (the year that Delaware County came into being) and the early 1900s. Newer information is stored at the Media Courthouse. No one seems to know where or how any of the court records, including the D'Amore court proceedings, are kept, so it is impossible to say whether any such records actually exist at this time. Another stumbling block is created because only one person, Helen Guanti, the sister of the two defendants, remains alive, and she has not spoken about the crime.

So in order to get an idea of what happened during the trial, I was left with various articles from three newspapers: the *Chester Times*, the *Philadelphia Evening Bulletin* and the *Philadelphia Inquirer*. Some articles present direct testimony while other articles present an overall view of the daily court proceedings. When the testimony was direct, I have presented it as such. When it was not, I have used the quotes and other recorded sources. I have made every attempt to tell the story of the trial as it happened.

Another issue that I feel may need some clarification is the legal definition of insanity. During the court proceedings, both the prosecution and the defense called expert witnesses to the stand. These witnesses were considered experts in the medical discipline of psychiatry. There is a considerable difference between the medical definition of insanity and the legal definition of insanity. It all comes down to two legal tests, one known as the M'Naghten Rule and the other known as the Irresistible Impulse

Test. According to the M'Naghten Rule, the defendant has to understand the nature and quality of whatever he or she does and if that act is right or wrong. The Irresistible Impulse Test says that even if a defendant knows right from wrong, the impulse to commit the crime may be so great that it overcomes that knowledge.[1] Of course, because of the lack of information regarding the trial, there is no way of knowing whether the experts used one or the other of these tests to reach their conclusions.

On the subject of testimony from experts, much has changed since 1950. It would seem that, back when the D'Amore case was being heard, there were very few legal questions concerning the qualifications of the experts. There is no record that either the prosecution or the defense challenged the skills, knowledge or procedure used by the experts. In actuality, the idea of challenges to expert witnesses would not become a legal issue until 1993 with the Daubert ruling.[2]

A note about spelling: I have found that Mrs. D'Amore's first name can be spelled two ways, Conchetta or Concetta. In my e-mail discussions with a source in Italy, the spelling Concetta is used. I have followed that lead.

I

THE SKELETON IN THE CLOSET AND THE LITTLE GIRL IN THE BASEMENT

A lot of families have those little family secrets that people talk about at holiday dinners or at weddings and funerals. Maybe Aunt Connie gets into the cooking sherry now and then when her husband is at work, or it could be that Uncle Jim ran away to join the carnival when he was just eighteen. Most of the time, these tales are much more humorous than they are embarrassing.

Occasionally, a skeleton is buried much deeper, in back of the closet, because it represents a family secret so damaging that it can rip apart trust and loyalty and leave hurt and misunderstanding as the family fabric tears apart. This is especially true when the secret has to do with a most horrific crime—murder—and even more when the murder is patricide.

Dawn D'Amore was born into a family that held that type of secret. It was a secret about abuse, dysfunction and two brothers, two of Dawn's uncles, who committed the most unspeakable of acts when they lay in ambush one winter's evening outside of their parents' home. As their father got out of the family car, they executed him in cold blood.

While this is the story of that crime, it is also the story of a little girl who knew something was wrong, who grew up in a family that kept their secret from her and who searched, and continues to search, for the answers as she grew into adulthood.

Most of the material that makes up this story has been collected by Dawn in an attempt to clear her mind and to come to grips with what happened to her grandfather back in 1949. It took years for her to find out what happened,

Fun on the tricycle. *By Sally Klann.*

and it took her down a road that she may not have wanted to travel. In the end, she learned about a history of abuse, both physical and mental, by her grandfather and other members of the D'Amore clan. She learned that her two uncles said that they had no alternative but to murder their father in order to get out from under his bullying and to save their mother's life.

Even now, however, Dawn carries a thought in the back of her mind that haunts her and keeps her unsure of the true motive of the crime; she remains unconvinced that her two uncles plotted the murder on their own, and she remains unconvinced that other members of the family were as uninvolved as they claim. Dawn continues to search for what really happened outside of her grandfather's home. To her, the real skeleton remains hidden in the deep, dark recesses of the D'Amore closet.

It is not unusual for children to find special places in which to play at home. Attics are fun places to cover your tracks during a good game of hide-and-seek; the garage makes for a great playhouse when the weather is nice enough to be outside; the basement can be a mysteriously enjoyable setting to conjure up ghosts and goblins among storage boxes and noisy heaters.

For young Dawn D'Amore, the basement was her place to enjoy playing with her sisters. Dressed in party clothes and Mary Jane shoes, she would ride her bike in circles around the water heater. To this day, Dawn says that she has fond memories of the time spent playing in the cellar. When it was time to nap, Dawn would climb up onto the workbench and fall asleep under a warm blanket that had been placed on her by her sister Bonnie.

But there was one thing about having a basement as a playroom in the D'Amore household that was really out of the ordinary. Once the children were down there, they could not get out. Both basement doors—the one at the top of the steps that led into the first-floor kitchen and the one that opened up into the back yard—were locked.

To the children, the basement was a great place to play, but to the adults seated around the kitchen table right above the kids, the basement was a secure chamber, a place to hold the sisters so they would not hear any talk of the murder of their grandfather.

For the most part, children are much smarter and much more intuitive than adults seem to think. It usually doesn't take children long to catch on if something doesn't seem right to them. Dawn was no exception. It didn't take long for her to put two and two together and figure out that every time her two uncles came by to talk with her father, she and her sisters ended up locked in the basement.

It's not unusual for kids to be curious, particularly when the adults are all sitting around the kitchen table talking in hushed voices about something. When her uncles would arrive at the house, Dawn would quietly climb the basement stairs and try to listen to the adults' conversations, but as she recalls, the talk was in whispers and very difficult to hear. She couldn't hear much, and what she did hear really did not make too much sense to her. As time went on and as the family conversations continued, Dawn's curiosity grew until, when she was twenty-three years old, she "got into her father's face" and demanded to know the truth. The truth, however, was even more alarming than she expected.

Even before she learned the truth about the family's secret, life was not easy for Dawn. She said, "At times, there was not much to eat. Sometimes all I had to eat was spice." It did not go without notice that no matter how long the D'Amore children went without, their father was always considered first in the mind of their mother. This seemed to be the pattern in their grandfather's home as well. Benjamin was always the primary member of the family, and the kids were always secondary.

Of course, this might have been simply a way to show respect to the head of the family. In many cultures, the husband, as breadwinner, is considered worthy of first-in-line consideration from his spouse. After all, the D'Amores were of Italian stock, and Dawn's grandfather and grandmother were immigrants from the Old Country. Also, this was a time when a woman's position in life was still subservient to that of the man, not only in the family setting but in the social arena as well.

Dawn has a different thought on this; she believes that both her grandfather and father held a superior position in the family more out of fear than respect. There is reason to believe, from stories told by her family members, that past generations of the D'Amore family suffered abuse, both mental and physical, at the hands of parents and siblings.

What is also interesting is that, in both her grandfather's family and in Dawn's family, one particular member acted as a surrogate abuser. In her grandfather's family, it was a sister, Helen; in Dawn's family, it was one of her sisters. Dawn recalled that while her father and mother never physically abused her, someone else would inflict the punishment. The beating came if Dawn did anything that would upset or annoy their mother. Dawn remembers that she was not the "golden child" or the favorite of her parents.

When Dawn's father finally spoke about the murder, he talked about how he had also been sent to the basement and, while there, was handcuffed as a form of punishment. The comparison to Dawn's time in the basement is striking, to be sure.

So it seems obvious that the members D'Amore family suffered from various types of abuse, and certainly, abuse can be a solid motivator for murder when all other means of escape fail, but in some cases, the real motive for a crime is hidden under a cloak of mystery. When it comes to homicide, one emotion can be even more telling than fear, and that emotion is greed. Is it at all possible that the real reason Benjamin D'Amore was executed by his two sons was the desire for the money, property and business that had made D'Amore a successful individual? Some, to this day, think so. The sons of Benjamin D'Amore said that they had to kill their father to save their mother, but they might have committed the crime to line their own pockets and the pockets of other family members. In any case, the D'Amore brothers, with the help of a brilliant move from their defense attorney, solved both problems and, in the end, found their pockets lined.

Writers of nonfiction describe facts that surround an event or a person. Facts do not show raw emotion or the stress that an event, especially a murder in a family, evokes in members of that family. Only the words of the family members can show what it is like to go through the years wondering why, how and what if. Dawn's own words do just that.

Dawn's Story

There are several parts of Dawn's story that are of a personal nature and do not have anything to do with her thoughts on the murder of her grandfather. I promised Dawn that I would edit out those sections. I have done that. Otherwise, the remainder of this chapter is in Dawn's words. The reader may conclude that some of the material therein is redundant, and the reader would be correct. Regarding that issue, I do not see it as my task to eliminate what Dawn has written. She collected all the facts over a long period of time, and they all became part of her search for the truth. My job was to look at the facts and see between the lines, so to speak. My task was to try to answer the whys of the D'Amore murder and how law enforcement and the judicial system played into the ultimate results. Also, there are some facts and comments that were told to Dawn directly by some family members. These facts do not appear in any other sources because they were for her ears only.

I was born on January 16, 1964, the eighth and last child of Anthony and Jessie D'Amore of Morton, Delaware County, Pennsylvania. They had six girls and two boys, and we lived in a three-bedroom house on Franklin Avenue. I don't remember a lot of my childhood; I blocked it out for some reason, I guess. The things I do remember I have questions about—some things were good, some were bad. I remember the most about being the poor kid, with my parents not paying no mind to what I was doing. I remember missing so much school, and yet no one came to see why or helped me. I always knew something wasn't right, or I felt like something or someone wasn't telling me something because I was so young. I would hear my father talk to his brothers in the kitchen and then hush when I came in the room. It seemed to be the place where important talks would be, and the table was long and many could fit around it. So as a kid, I would listen to find out what was going on. And I would think it was so odd that I had two aunts on my father's side but they never came over. And when my dad would take us to their house, my mom would never come. So I knew there was a secret, I just couldn't figure it out, so I started listening more and asking my dad but got little bits and pieces.

A good memory I had of my childhood was being down in the basement and riding my tricycle around the heater in my black Mary Janes and being all dressed up. Even when I think of it now, I get a smile on my face. Once, my sister and I were talking about memories, and how I don't have many. When she heard that this was one that makes me happy, she said, "You don't remember, do you?" Then she told me why we were down in the basement. You see, my dad would lock us down there as he had his talks in the kitchen; to him, he was keeping us safe. She told me that when I got tired, she would make me a bed on the workbench and cover me with Christmas stuff to keep me warm. And as soon as she said it, I could see it—I remembered. And all kinds of things started to come back, but just in pieces.

My father was a truck driver, and my mom was a homemaker. My dad was only home three days out of the week because he drove out west and back a lot, and my mom went to bingo three days a week. They seemed to be the days he was home. I remember being hungry, and when dad came home, she would feed him before she left, but there was nothing for us. I always thought it was because we were poor, but if that were the case, how could she go to bingo so much? She ate there. I know because I used to walk up and watch her play. I was four or five years old, and I was walking the streets alone looking for someone to keep me company or even to invite me for dinner, which my one friend Mary's parents did and did it often. But that stopped. I was six and so afraid. She hated me, and I loved her, or maybe I just liked that someone cared for me, which she had 'til this. So I felt like I lost my adopted family, which was four houses down from mine. I wasn't allowed there, but sometimes I would see Mary outside and we would play.

Where was I to go now? I felt so alone and hungry, so I decided to run away. There were train tracks out back of our house, so I walked down, then I found a little fort and stayed. I was there for a couple days 'til it started raining real bad, and the thunder was so loud. As I was running home, I thought they would be happy to see me, sweep me up in their arms and tell me they loved me, but no, they didn't even know I was gone. So now what could I do? How could I get them to see I was alive? I rebelled and got angry and got in as much trouble as I could, and now I was getting some attention. And at that time, one of my family members got married at a young age. Her and her new husband moved in, and their son was born, and my mom was so happy. They made a bedroom for them out of the dinning room. It was a good idea since we didn't use it. And then, baby number two was on its way, and Donna and her husband moved to an apartment. Since I was on a bad streak, I would get in my dad's face and ask what are the secrets about the family, why are my cousins living so great and we are such dirty little secrets? Again, I got bits and pieces. My mom couldn't handle me; she would get so mad at me, start to tell me stuff and then stop. This is when my life as I knew it changed.

She sent me to babysit Donna's babies when Donna and her hubby would go out. And they went out a lot, so I stayed there for weeks at a time. They began leaving me alone with the babies more and more. I was so scared in that apartment. Then one day, they moved to a bigger place. I was so happy, and they started to treat me like I was a teenager and party with me. I was now nine years old. I now know that they partied with me to get me to stay and watch the kids more. I was alone for a week or more at a time with the kids no with no phone, food or car.

'Til one day, my mom showed up and was so upset. The school was worried that I hadn't been going; finally someone cared. She went in to see the principal and was told that if I made up my work and went to school, things would be fine. So now here I am with my mom and my sister doing my homework. And yes, they were doing the homework papers too because there was so much. I went back home and went to school for a couple of weeks, and it all kept happening all over again. It became routine: babysit, be alone, and then we all do my homework and then back to school again for a couple weeks.

'Til the drugs and the drinking and fights became too much. I couldn't handle what was going on around me.

My other sister Bonnie moved in with my parents while I was gone. Actually, her and her husband and young daughter moved in to help my parents with the bills. My parents lost the house, and they bought it. And they all lived together. Bonnie was close to my dad; she always looked out for him. And the weeks when I would come home, Bonnie would help me with my homework—not by doing it, but by teaching me. I was so happy when I was with her, and I loved that I was learning things. It was exciting, and I was doing good, and I was happy to be normal. But I would have to leave again and watch the kids and see things that a young girl shouldn't have to. Bonnie is the one person that made me feel like I was loved and smart. I was missing her. I couldn't handle the parties and stuff that were going on right in front of me. And the kids—I couldn't escape. They would just have me drink and smoke weed and do pills; I was so high. And in my head, I thought this was great. But it was just a way people had a hold of me so I wouldn't leave because they would tell on me. I should have let her, she was my sister and my party pal, and we were close. But I was so young and stupid. I didn't know how I could get out of this. I was scared that one of her party friends, mostly guys, would hurt me. They already tried to get me to have sex with them, but I didn't. I was terrified. I wanted to go home even though it wasn't my home. I don't ever feel like I had a home 'til I married. I missed my friends at school and hanging out with them and doing bad things, as kids did. I felt so much older than them because of the things I had seen and done.

I missed Bonnie; she was like a mother to me. She packed me lunches for school, and I always had dinner with her when I was home. I just couldn't figure out how to get out of what was going on or how my parents could let it, so I ran away. A friend got me a bus ticket, and I went to the shore. I was now free and twelve years old. After rough nights sleeping on the beach, almost three weeks later, I was homesick, so I called my mom. She told me to come home only because the friend who had bought me the ticket and was still with me had stolen the money from their dad. My mom wanted me to get my friend home because their parents were bugging them to find us. She didn't even seem worried about me, just worried about the other parents bugging her. Anyway, I wanted to go home. I was tired and hungry and needed a bath and needed a hug. When I got off the bus at the Sixty-ninth Street terminal in Upper Darby, my mom and my relatives were there. I got my ass beat right then and there. I think mostly so the other parent would see, and to blame it all on me and plus for my mom. She threw me in the truck, and home we went. It started a big fight, and mom sent me home with a relative. Two weeks later, after Donna came home from work, she let me out to hang with my friends I had met at her apartment. Everything was fine, and it got late, so I went in. Donna and her husband were fighting, and they fought a lot, and she would always tell me to leave and come back later. So now here I am walking the streets, and a guy pulled up to me that I had met at Donna's apartment before. He asked what I was doing, so I told him. He told me to come over to his place because it was chilly out and watch some TV and that he would take me back in an hour—things most likely would be calm by then. So I went, but why was I so stupid again? Why did I trust him? Because he partied at Donna's place often, so I thought it was OK?

He beat me so bad that the ring he was wearing left imprints all over my face, back and chest. And he raped me. I felt worthless. When I had the chance, I ran. And he chased me 'til some other man on the street heard what was going on and told me to call my mom, and then he called the police. I was so scared to go in his house, but there was a girl there who helped me. They even drove me to the hospital.

The next day, my dad and my Uncle Johnny sat me at the big table in the kitchen and told me that with the way the court was and how developed I was, it would look like I asked for this to happen to me. I was so scared, even more scared that I was at the kitchen table where the secrets were told. They told me they would handle it. And my mom had a bag packed, and they sent me to stay with my sister Judy. Judy and her husband lived very well—nice house, nice family life. As I was there, her husband freaked when he came home from work, saying I was trash. And I heard Judy telling him to be quiet, that I would hear him. He didn't care. He came right up to my face and told me he wanted me out. I never did anything to this man; I couldn't understand why he hated me so much. I already felt like trash.

So this was it. I quit!

I ran away again, but this time, I promised myself to take control of my life the best I could because me, myself, was all I had.

My mom and my sister Bonnie got in a fight, so my parents moved to a house a couple blocks away that they rented and had Donna and her husband and kids move in, too. I was so done with Donna. All I did was fight with her; punches flew many times. I was still a nobody to my family. I had to share the attic with Donna's kids. It was nice, but why couldn't I have my own room like my sister Amy did? I became so lost, and then I turned wild. I mean, why not? No one cared. I met a boy during this time. His parents had just broken up, but he had a home. It was nice, and we hung out there. For the first time, I had someone who made me feel good, even though we were young and wild. I started to like my life.

So six months later, my parents had a fight with Donna and moved again and took Amy and myself with them. Amy is four years older than me, but never had to go through or see what I had to. She was considerd pure and innocent, and I was always reminded of that. We lived very different lives. And I was the bad one, and everyone let me know that.

So at thirteen, my mom took me out of school because I kept skipping. And the school let her; she said she needed me at home to help her because she was diabetic. I mean, I was doing bad things, but I didn't hurt or steal from anyone. This was the only way I knew how to be—a party girl.

At fourteen, I became pregnant with the one boy who I gave myself to and moved out. I was so done with them not caring, and I did everything to get them to just notice me. I gave birth to a beautiful baby girl two months shy of my fifteenth birthday. I did move back with my parents twice because I needed their help, and stayed a couple months each time so my baby girl would have a place to sleep. But then, one day, I left and had to grow up. I know my parents loved me, but so many questions caused us to butt heads.

My daughter's father and I lasted for eight years. We just weren't meant to be, plus a baby and everything at such a young age was hard. And I was realizing how I didn't have a childhood or even a chance to be a teenager. I love my daughter and wanted her to have a family life without all the fighting. So I moved in with my now husband and had two sons.

When I was twenty-three and had my third child and was married, I had this overwhelming need to know how my parents could have done the things they had to me. I was looking at my daughter, thinking I could never have done this to her. So now, I wanted answers, and I wanted them now. I went over to their apartment and started asking again, bits and pieces, but a little more than before. So I kept pushing and telling my dad how wrong he had done me—for way more reasons than I have listed here. I wanted answers, and I wasn't leaving 'til I got some. And that is when he told me about his childhood. His father was a wife beater and used to beat him and his siblings and chain him and his brothers up in the basement. And he met my mom but went in the army only to be sent home because his father was killed.

My dad's family had money and owned a farm in Marple Township, Pennsylvania. He had two sisters and two brothers, and he was the youngest. They had a rough life with their dad, but when they got older, they enjoyed their family's money, cars, girls and food. But someone plotted to kill his father, and he thought it was for the money, not what his sisters and brothers and mom were saying—and I agree. After hearing it all, I think it was for the money.

One day when my grandfather came home, he was shot several times as soon as he got out of his car—in his own driveway, by his own two sons (my Uncle Johnny and Uncle Nick).

It was the biggest court case in Delaware County and made the newspapers everyday. The jury was made up of all women who had listened to the case. My uncles pleaded not guilty and said they did it because of the abuse. And they were acquitted because they didn't know which bullet in my grandfather had killed him.

To me, wouldn't that be premeditated murder? They waited and had it all planned out. After they were cleared, their lawyer asked the judge if he could kiss the jurors, and he was granted that request.

OK, who got paid off? That is my thought now.

So I went home and talked to my husband about all this, and he was shocked. He knew from hearing the family tell stories, but he just thought we were all full of shit, so he told me to not believe it. But I couldn't, and I needed more answers. So the next morning, I called Media Courthouse, and I wanted to read the transcripts. I was on hold for almost half hour, and she said they were burned. OK, so now what? She told me she could tell me the verdict, and it was just like my dad had said: acquitted. So I called my dad and told him I was shocked, and why keep it a secret that his father was murdered? And he said he didn't want his brothers to go to jail. Somehow, with all this, my dad never returned to the army again. Who got paid off, again? I wonder what he could have been, and my mom not having to be treated like crap from his sister Helen. Wait, now I had another question: why was my mom getting treated that way? And I asked my dad with my mom there. He started to tell me but stopped when he looked at my mom. And she said it was all about my aunt Helen, Aunt Nellie as I knew her. And that was all I got for years. 'Til the day I got all the details I could, even down to the names and addresses of the jurors. At this time, I lived in upstate Pennsylvania, three hours away. I told my husband we had to come down home to visit my family. I was on the hunt for the rest of this story.

And my dad gave in some more but made me promise to never tell 'til Uncle Johnny had passed away. Here we go again—secrets. Well, Uncle Johnny passed away in the summer of 2010, so here is my family secret in my findings through old microfilm from newspapers.

On the night of November 20, 1949, Benjamin D'Amore, fifty-three-year-old Marple Township nurseryman, pulled into his driveway. As his headlights shined on the garage door, he got out of the car to open the garage, and shots were fired and blasted away part of his head and killed him. The shots were fired by his own sons Nicholas, twenty-six, who lived on Jefferson Street near Fifty-third, and John, twenty-two, who lived on Parkside Avenue near Forty-ninth.

The headlines on November 21, 1949, in the *Evening Bulletin* read, "Sons Kill Father, Charge He Beat Crippled Mother." The *Philadelphia Inquirer*'s headlines said, "2 Sons Slay Father, Say He Beat Mother."

The *Evening Bulletin* said the two sons blasted a shotgun and deer rifle shortly before 11:00 p.m. The top of their father's head was torn off by the blasts.

R. Paul Lessy, assistant district attorney, said the two sons surrendered immediately and confessed to the slaying. Both brothers were charged with murder but pleaded not guilty during the brief preliminary hearing before Marple Township justice of peace Ernest Dupille the next morning. They were held without bail.

Later that day, their attorney, Albert Blumberg, secured a writ of habeas corpus in a move seeking their release from jail. Judge Harold I. Ervin of Delaware County's Common Pleas Court granted the preliminary writ and set a hearing for 10:00 a.m. the next morning.

The sons told Lessy that they found their mother, Conecetta, fifty-two, in tears when they arrived about 6:00 p.m. to borrow an electric fan. They said their mother told them her husband had "beat her up again."

The mother's left arm, leg and side had been paralyzed since an illness about two years before. The beating, according to the dead man's partner and son-in-law John Guanti, followed an argument over a pair of socks.

The father left the house and drove off in his new sedan. When Nicholas and John dropped in, their mother showed them her bruised face.

Lessy said Nicholas told him, "We decided we'd kill the old man—that tonight was the night. I sent John to my house to get the rifle. I knew that my father had a shotgun in the house, but I wanted two guns—I didn't want him to get away."

When John returned about 8:00 p.m., the brothers loaded both weapons and stood in the driveway near the house, about four hundred feet off State Road. They waited for their father to drive back home.

"The plan was this," Nicholas continued, "I was going to shoot first, and if I didn't kill him with that first bullet, John was to fire the shotgun."

The father drove up to the garage, unaware that his sons were in the shadows about thirty feet away. He got out of the car and walked toward the garage door, his figure silhouetted by the headlights.

"I fired but missed," Nicholas was quoted as saying. "He started to run around the front of the car, and I fired again. It hit him this time. Afterward, I went over and looked at him and knew he was dead. Then, we went back to the house to wait for the police."

The other brother, John, corroborated Nicholas's story, Lessy said, adding that he fired the shotgun when the first rifle bullet missed its target. The preliminary examination failed to show whether one or both weapons were responsible for the fatal head wound, Fred Jack, chief of county detectives, said. An autopsy was held.

The slain man was survived by three other children, Guanti's estranged wife, Helen, twenty-seven; Yolanda DiMaggio, twenty-five, of Upper Darby; and Anthony, nineteen, a soldier stationed in Mississippi.

The *Philadelphia Inquirer* said mostly the same thing but had some additional information. The November 21, 1949 newspaper said that the two sons were charged for the murder and had confessed, and that they did it because of the beating their mother had received.

"I waited for years to do this—since I was six," District Attorney R. Paul Lessy quoted the eldest son as saying. "He was always abusing Mother. I knew this was the end…I didn't want him to get away."

The detective said Nicholas and John had dropped in earlier to visit their mother, Concetta, and were told by brother-in-law John Guanti that "Dad beat Mom again."

"It was over a pair of socks," Guanti was quoted as saying. "The old man wanted to wear a certain pair that hadn't been washed yet. He gave her quite a going-over."

The sons were so incensed that they picked up their deer rifle and shotgun and posted themselves at the front window, awaiting their father's return. When his shiny new car turned into the driveway leading to the garage beside the house, the two sons went out the rear door. When Benjamin D'Amore, their father, stepped out of the car, he was blasted to death instantly.

Guanti called the police of both Springfield and Marple Townships—Patrolmen Clarence Orr and Joseph Baker of Springfield, Patrolman Newton Kerber of Marple and Marple police chief Lester Downs.

The officers said Nicholas and John greeted them with a simple announcement: "We shot our father." The sons were taken first to Springfield Township police headquarters. Fred Jack, chief of Delaware County detectives, was preparing to transfer them to the Delaware County Courthouse in Media for formal questioning.

About one hundred yards from the tragedy scene, Harry Meyers, criminologist and former teacher in the Pennsylvania State Police School at Hershey, was sitting in his cottage dictating a manuscript to his secretary, Ms. Frances Willard of Larchmont.

"I heard shots," Meyers said. "My curiosity was aroused just enough to cause me to step outside. I saw the two young men walking back toward the house."

"'What's up?' I asked them.

"'Oh, nothing now,' one of the boys said. 'Everything's OK now!'

"So I let it go at that and returned to my dictations of a manuscript on the subject of crime."

Sometime later, the arrival of police gave Meyers his first indication of what happened.

Mrs. D'Amore, who suffers partailparalysis of an arm and a leg, apparently was sitting in the kitchen with Guanti when the shooting occurred, police said.

The two sons were married, and one had a small child. Nicholas was employed by the Budd Co. and John by the American Forestry Service landscaping contractors, Lancaster Pike near City Line, Overbrook.

A brother, Anthony was a soldier stationed in Mississippi. The D'Amore sons also had two sisters—Guanti's wife, Helen, twenty-seven, and Mrs. Yolanda DiMaggio, twenty-three, of Upper Darby.

Mr. and Mrs. Guanti were separated. Guanti, associated with the D'Amores in the operation of the nursery, continued living with Mr. and Mrs. D'Amore. He said he believed Mrs. Guanti was in Philadelphia. When his wife left home about a year earlier, Guanti had reported her missing and told police she "couldn't get along with her father."

On November 22, 1949, in an articled titled "Bail Denied 2 Who Slew Their Father in Ambush," the *Philadelphia Inquirer* reported:

> *The two brothers are sent to Broadmeadows Farm Prison yesterday without bail to await the action of the next Delaware County grand jury. Both were silent as they were arraigned on homicide charges before Justice of the Peace Ernest Dupille, in Broomall Delaware County.*
>
> *Details of the ambush shooting of Benjamin P. D'Amore, fifty-three—owner of the State Road Nurseries, State Road, Marple Township—were supplied by Lester Downs, police chief of Marple Township. The hearing before Dupille was brief and came after two brothers, neither displaying any remorse, had been questioned throughout the early morning hours by Assistant District Attorney R. Paul Lessy and Fred Jack, chief of Delaware County detectives.*
>
> *On the advice of their attorney Albert Blumberg, Chester, the two brothers remained silent after pleading not guilty to the murder charges. As the hearing ended, Blumberg announced he would ask Delaware County Court to grant bail for the two brothers through habeas corpus writs.*
>
> *The two brothers had a short, tearful reunion with their mother on their way to prison. Jack and Downs acceded to their wishes that they be allowed to see their mother before they were locked up.*

THE D'AMORE FAMILY TRAGEDY

Mrs. D'Amore, whose left side arm and leg had been paralyzed for about two years, had been near collapse since the murder of her husband about 11:00 p.m. on November 20, 1949. She was even more perturbed after seeing her sons taken away to prison.

John Guanti, the dead man's business partner and son-in-law who lived at the D'Amore home, estranged from his wife, Helen, told investigators there had been an argument over a pair of socks, and D'Amore had beaten his wife before driving off in his new sedan.

Fourteen married women—most of them mothers and some grandmothers—were chosen at Media for the jury to try Nicholas W. and John D'Amore, my uncles, in Delaware County Court for the murder of their father, my grandfather, Benjamin P. D'Amore, fifty-three, owner of the State Road Nurseries in Marple Township.

If the jury seemed a little out of the ordinary, so also was the courtroom scene in which the brothers pleaded not guilty and waited for the trial to get under way. Not only were the two sisters, Aunt Helen and Aunt Yolanda, and another brother, my dad, there, but their mother, my grandmother, also sat with them at the time.

According to a confession quoted by Assistant District Attorney R. Paul Lessy, the two brothers admitted slaying their father with blasts from a shotgun and a deer rifle because he had repeatedly beaten their crippled mother, Concetta, fifty-two, whose left arm and left side had been paralyzed since an illness two years ago.

The two surrendered immediately after the slaying on November 20, and Lessy, at the time, said they readily admitted to the patricide. He said they told of ambushing their father a little before eleven o'clock that night as he stepped from his car to unlock the garage door at his home on State Road near Sproul, adjoining the nursery.

As he questioned prospective jurors, Lessy indicated that he would ask for a first-degree murder verdict with the death penalty. There was no effort to have the two defendants tried separately. After pleas were entered before Judge William R. Toal, the brothers' attorney, Albert Blumberg, waived their right to a separate trial.

The patricide trial started on January 2, 1950.

Statements in which Nicholas and John D'Amore said they had been "figuring" ever since they were boys that someday they might have to kill their father were admitted as evidence at the Media Courthouse during the second day of the brothers' patricide trial in Delaware County Court.

Each statement, admitted over the strenuous objection of Albert Blumberg, defense counsel, told of years in which the father, Benjamin P. D'Amore, had beaten and kicked his wife, now a cripple—years that culminated on the night of November 20, when the two brothers, according to their statements, blasted away part of their father's head at his Marple Township nursery after seeing the latest evidence of his mistreatment.

Assistant District Attorney R. Paul Lessy asked the all-female jury to find the defendants guilty of murder.

Although Albert Blumsburg lost his fight to bar the statements on the grounds that they were obtained under "psychological duress," he did succeed, once the state had rested, in having the conspiracy indictment against his clients quashed. The court ruled that the only evidence of conspiracy was in the two brothers' statements, which would not be accepted as such when the state could offer nothing in support.

Only one blast, but neither knew which gun it had come from, had dropped their victim. Nicholas, twenty-six, said in his statement that he was six years old when he first got the idea that "eventually" he would have to kill his father "because of the way he treated all of us." His brother John said the idea first occurred to him when he was eight. According to John's statement, he had left his father's home and employment three or four weeks before the slaying "because he was always hollering at somebody or hitting somebody."

The two statements tallied in the brothers' account of how they happened to enter the Marple Township house only a minute or two after their father had left, how they found their mother moaning and crying after the latest beating and how they knew then, as Nicholas put it, that "this is it."

John was sent to Nicholas's house on Jefferson Street near Fifty-third to get the rifle because they were afraid of using just their father's shotgun and missing. John lived on Parkside Avenue near Forty-ninth Street. When the younger brother returned, they loaded the weapons and waited for their father's return.

As their father stepped from his car and started to unlock the garage, according to statements, Nicholas fired first with the rifle and missed. Then, as their father turned, he reloaded and shot again. John fired.

Dr. Vincent A. Nacrelli, coroner's physician, testified that he was unable to tell which weapon fired the fatal charge. Chief county detective Fred Jack, under cross-examination, said he found Mrs. D'Amore that night with a large bruise on her left cheek.

Mrs. D'Amore, paralyzed in her left arm and side since a stroke two years earlier, sat with her sons during the day's session, except for one moment in which her emotions overcame her and she had to be led out of the courtroom.

The start of Blumberg's formal defense precipitated an argument when he said he would prove that, over a long period of time, the father's treatment of his family had built up a resentment that exploded the night of November 20.

With the jury out of the room, it was argued by the prosecution that such a line of testimony would not be admissible. In the end, the court ruled that the defense could offer whatever testimony it wanted but that such background evidence could be considered by the jury only in fixing the penalty, in the event the verdict was guilty.

NICHOLAS AND JOHN ADMITTED to an all-female jury that they fired the shots that killed their father after he had administered the last of innumerable beatings to their crippled mother. Both denied they had planned the killing or were aware of what had happened 'til it was accomplished. While the female jurors listened with unconcealed horror, both young men told of the grim life that was all they could remember since they were small boys, of being cruelly beaten themselves and seeing their mother beaten almost daily—for things the children had done or had not done—by a sadistic father.

Their stories corroborated and amplified those told by their fifty-two-year-old mother, Mrs. Concetta D'Amore, who brought the trial to a climax in its third day. However, both were caught in cross-examination by the one key discrepancy between their statements to police and the witness stand—whether the killing was planned. They insisted there was no premeditation, whatever they had said when first taken into custody.

In their pre-trial statements, the brothers had said they had "figured" for years that, someday, they would have to kill their father for his abusive treatment of their mother.

Nicholas, the first of the brothers to take the stand, sobbed so convulsively that, for a time, it was difficult for the court stenographers to hear what he said. From the time he was five years old, he said, the children and mother had known nothing but continuous mistreatment from their father.

"My first day of school, I got afraid for some reason and ran home. When my father asked my mother why I wasn't in school and she told him, he grabbed her and started beating her. He bumped her head against the wall, and when she fell, he kicked her. When I got a poor report card, he would beat me and Mom both and tell her it was her fault.

"He would often chain me to a post in the cellar overnight without any food. When he caught my mom bringing down food to me, he would beat her."

Before going to school, the boys had to get up at daybreak and work on the thirty-acre property that the nursery business occupied. And when they came home, they had to work late into the night. John told much the same story of frequent beatings as his brother had, but in a more composed voice.

"I would be so sleepy in school, I would doze over my lessons and then the teacher would send a note home, and he would beat me and Mom for that, too. When I was fourteen, he put me in the cellar for nearly two weeks to punish me for something, and he told me, 'You deserve to sleep with the rats.'"

He and his brother, who had left home as soon as the outbreak of war gave them a chance to enter the army, had gone to live in Philadelphia some time before the killing. On that night, they testified, they drove up to see their mother and found her crying and moaning. Her husband had just beat her again and left the house.

Nicholas sent John to the former's home for a rifle, but John testified he didn't know why his brother wanted the weapon. When John returned, he went upstairs and got his father's shotgun because, he said, he "wanted to hide it so my father couldn't get it when he came home."

When they heard the car in the driveway, Nicholas said he was the first to run out.

"I grabbed the rifle and ran out," he said. "My father was walking in front of his car toward the garage. I started shaking with nerves, and I fired a shot. I didn't see him anymore, and I ran back in the house."

This did not take account of the other shot fired by John, who said he came out just behind Nicholas. John said he saw Nicholas's rifle go up and heard it shoot.

"I got scared, and my gun went off. There was another shot, and I saw my father fall down. Then, we went back into the house."

Mrs. D'Amore's testimony, given without tears but with expressive movements of her good hand, was so intense in its quiet horror that Judge William R. Toal repeatedly had to order his court officers to silence the female jurors' gasps. He could do nothing about their tears, but he cautioned the jurors that they must not let the mother's story sway them in determining the sons' guilt or innocence. It must be considered, he said, only in determining the degree of guilt if a guilty verdict were found.

The gray-haired Mrs. D'Amore, who took the stand in the morning, summed up her whole unhappy story with the statement: "He beat me all the time. He started when the kids were very young. Every day, he beat me."

Taking of testimony in the case of Nicholas and his brother John for the murder of their father entered its closing phase on January 8, 1950. The Commonwealth of Pennsylvania called rebuttal witnesses when the court resumed that day, the defense having rested after a short session on Saturday night.

Attorneys for the D'Amore brothers, accused of slaying their father, were expected to call a few rebuttal witnesses, and then, the counsel for each side would present closing arguments.

The jury, after receiving a final summation from Judge William R. Toal, was expected to begin its deliberations early the next week. Two daughters, my aunt Helen and aunt Yolanda, and a third son, Tony, my father, were called as the last defense witnesses to support the contention of the defendants that they shot their father because of his brutal treatment of his family.

One of the latter witnesses was questioned at length by Judge Toal. One jurist interrupted questioning of Mrs. Helen Bolenski (my aunt), twenty-four years old, of Lima, Delaware County, who had told of severe beatings administered by her father to herself and her mother. She was asked what her father had used to strike his victims. Judge Toal was told a belt buckle and his fists. On one hand, the witness said, her father had worn a heavy ring that frequently caused painful bruises. In answer to another question by Judge Toal, she said that none of them was ever knocked unconscious, had any bones broken or had required hospitalization.

After Judge Toal remarked that he could not understand how Mr. Benjamin D'Amore's beatings, if they were so severe, had never caused injuries serious enough to require medical treatment. Albert Blumberg, defense attorney, objected to the jurist's questions. He was granted an exception.

Mrs. Yolanda DiMaggio, my aunt, of Upper Darby, another daughter, and Anthony, my father, D'Amore's third son, took the stand briefly to confirm the testimony of other members of the family.

The fate of Nicholas and John, accused of patricide, was placed in the hands of a jury of twelve mothers in Delaware County Criminal Court in Media at 8:45 p.m. on January 9, 1950. A death penalty verdict was ruled out by the prosecutor a few hours before the jurors took the case. Defense witnesses in the five-day trial had maintained that Mr. Benjamin P. D'Amore beat his partially crippled wife and their children for years.

Judge William R. Toal told the jurors, during a charge lasting one and three-quarters hours, that it would not be wise to give immediate consideration to their verdict. "Get a good night's rest tonight," he said, "and begin thinking what the verdict should be tomorrow."

Helen and Anthony calming Concetta. *By Sally Klann.*

The judge told the jurors they could return a verdict of first- or second-degree murder, manslaughter or acquittal. He said the case hinged on the jury's evaluation of testimony by four psychiatrists—two of them defense witnesses, who called the brothers temporarily insane when their father was slain with a shotgun and deer rifle, and the other state witnesses, who called them sane.

"There is no dispute that these boys killed their father," Judge Toal pointed out in his charge. "The real question is: What was their mental state at the time of the killing? If, after thorough deliberation, you conclude that the defendants were insane, your verdict will be 'not guilty' by reason of insanity. On the other hand, if you find they were capable of knowing right from wrong and there was premeditation and there is no reasonable doubt, you will find them guilty of murder in the first degree. The law does not justify killing because of rage, and an individual can't take the law in his own hands. If the law permitted it, civilization would revert to barbarism."

Earlier in the day, Assistant District Attorney R. Paul Lessy, in his summation, had told the jury, "This case does not demand the extreme penalty of death. Anyone not affected by that testimony of cruelty would be less than human," he said.

Nevertheless, he went on to say that the two brothers killed their father "willfully and with premeditation," and first-degree murder was the only possible verdict.

Having saved his clients at least from the chair, Albert Blumberg, defense counsel, called for complete acquittal, "not [for] sympathy, but on the merits of this case. Death has gone out the window, and I'm hopeful that, by the time this is finished, the entire case will be out the window."

Lessy's summation toward the close of the fifth day of the trial revealed that he had reached a decision not to ask for the death penalty at 3:30 a.m. on Sunday after having reviewed every word of the previous week's testimony. At the same time, he added, he was not at all sure that the accounts of the father's cruelty had not been exaggerated.

"Suppose it has been exaggerated," replied Blumberg when his turn came. "Take off 90 percent of it, and that alone will convince you ladies of the jury what hell there must have been in that Marple Township household all those years."

Then, pointing at Mrs. Concetta D'Amore, the crippled mother who sat at the counsel table with her sons, Blumberg continued, "Were the lines on the woman's face caused by her fifty-two years or by her unbearable suffering? How many years of tears were needed to give her eyes that sorrowful look? Yet she still proudly has the love that her sons give her. The one unusual thing about this murder case is that nobody has shed any tears over the deceased. His epitaph should be: 'He won't beat Mom any more.'"

Throughout the trial, it had been contended that if there was such a history of cruelty, someone should have gone to the authorities and made an effort to have it stopped. The day before, as a rebuttal witness for the defense, Harvey W. Williamson, chief of the township police, had testified that the brothers twice had visited him to ask what could be done about their father's brutality. Before the state closed its case, two psychiatrists were put on the stand to contradict the testimony of two specialists who, the previous Friday, had said the brothers were in a "catathymic crisis" on the night of November 20. It was explained in that testimony that persons in such a condition did not know right from wrong.

Both Dr. Charles Rupp and Dr. Joseph C. Yaskin from the University of Pennsylvania said, in their opinions, the brothers did indeed know right from wrong at the time of the murder. Dr. Rupp said the general theory of catathymic crisis had never received adequate substantiation.

NICHOLAS AND JOHN D'AMORE were found not guilty in the Delaware County Court at Media by the jury of twelve mothers who had tried them for their father's murder. The verdict was the signal for a demonstration of emotion equally as stirring as that which had pervaded nearly six days of trial. The widow wept on the shoulders of her sons. The defense attorney kissed each juror in turn. The judge shook hands with the two defendants, and the prosecutor told them both to be "good boys from here on in."

But that was nothing compared to the tearful congratulations the tightly knit D'Amore family both gave and received. Judge Willaim R. Toal might well have saved his warning against an outburst. The three hundred spectators jammed into the room were in a mood for applause.

Having received the case the night before, the all-mother jury began deliberating immediately after breakfast and reached their verdict in two hours and fifteen minutes. The large crowd had collected between noon, when the jury sent out word of an agreement, and 12:18 p.m., when the verdict was announced.

The forewoman, Mrs. Edith Force, failed to amplify the verdict in any way, nor did any of her sister jurors when they were polled by the clerk. So there was nothing to indicate whether the jurors considered the brothers to have been insane, at least for the moment when they blasted their father, Benjamin P. D'Amore, fifty-three, with a shotgun and rifle.

The judge had told them in his charge that the only legal question for them to decide was the defendants' sanity. He cautioned them against considering the testimony of the brutal wife beating that culminated in tragedy the night of November 20, 1949, except as a means of fixing the degree of guilt.

John and Nicholas, who, at twenty-six, is four years older then his co-defendant, sat almost impassive as the court began to address the jury. Their mother had been hunched over as if in prayer when the jury filed in. Now, it seemed to be taking quite a while for the verdict to sink in. Judge Toal began by telling the jurors that it had been a difficult case, that he knew they had tried hard to see both sides and bring in a fair verdict. But he did not say it was a fair one.

"I told the jurors this was an unlawful killing," said the judge, "and I still say so because the law never justifies a killing. Under the law, only a lunatic can be excused for murder. But over the best thirty years, a new idea has developed, which was expounded to you during this trial. This theory was developed by the two psychiatrists for the defense [Drs. M.A. Ornsteen and Gabriel Schwartz] and it is good that we have new ideas."

If Judge Toal's enthusiasm was conspicuously restrained, however, the joy of the brother's counsel, Albert Blumberg, knew no bounds. "They're wonderful," he exclaimed as he asked Judge Toal's permission to kiss the jurors. The judge replied in a matter-of-fact voice, " It's OK with the court."

Once that was accomplished, Blumberg led his clients up to the bench, where Judge Toal leaned over and shook their hands. "You've had a fair trial," he said. "The jury said you were not guilty. Now go home and be good boys."

The same admonishment was repeated by Assistant District Attorney R. Paul Lessy when he shook hands with Blumberg, his associate Mervin R. Turk and the now broadly smiling D'Amore brothers, who promptly took the advice. Together with their mother, crippled Mrs. Concetta D'Amore, fifty-three, the acquitted defendants went outside and posed for pictures with their sister Mrs. Helen Bolenski; a younger brother, my father, Anthony; and other members of the family.

Afterward, the slain man's former son-in-law John Guanti took the acquitted men back home on State Road near Sproul in Marple Township, the scene of the crime.

So WHY WAS THIS SUCH a secret in my family if the law freed them on the charges? Then what was the problem? I showed my dad my findings and asked him why he couldn't talk about it? All he said was how and where did I find it. I told him that it took some time, but for some reason, I needed to know why, for my whole life, I felt like I had this secret I was hiding with my family. And I hated the way it made me feel. I must have heard something when I was young that made me wonder. I don't know. My dad wouldn't talk about it but asked me to not publish it 'til my Uncle Johnny had passed away, since Uncle Nick was already passed. I said to him, "What do you mean publish? I'm no writer." He just asked that I wouldn't show it to anyone, and I told him I wouldn't if he would someday talk to me about it. I still needed some answers. Things didn't sit right with me. He said, "Why do you care?" I said, "Because the secret has something dirty to it, and I felt that my whole life."

It was a couple years later I was down visiting family again and when I saw my dad, for some reason, I brought up the subject again. And this time, he talked some, and I think it was because I asked him who got paid off. He asked what did I mean, and I said, "Who got paid off to free my uncles and why was it an all-female jury?" I never heard of that. He told me he didn't know much, but my aunt Helen would be able to tell me everything.

My aunt Helen was married to John Guanti and divorced him and married John Bolenski sometime before or right after the murder took place. But after the murder and when things calmed down, she divorced John Bolenski and remarried John Guanti. This was something I never knew, and I thought it was kinda weird that I didn't. And then, my dad wouldn't tell me anything else and got mad. So I thought this might have something to do with why my mom and Aunt Helen didn't get along. So I let it go for now.

A while went by, and when we would come down and visit, it was nice to see everyone. I didn't have any of them 'til I grew up. I mean, they were there, but not. Now, I was fitting in for the first time, and it was nice. I didn't bug my dad about the secret anymore since he got upset the last time we talked. And I liked that we could just be in the same room for now. At this time, I haven't see my aunt Yolanda since I was maybe eleven, and the last time I saw Aunt Helen, I was with my dad over at her house with my kids and hubby picking up a couch she gave me. I was twenty-four. Before that, the last time I had seen her, I was sixteen. The only uncle I could say I was close to was Uncle Nicky. Gosh, I loved him. I would go over there, and he would treat me like a princess—have his wife, Aunt Mel, make me something to eat, and she would show me how to cook. They had a daughter, but she was older, and I never really saw her 'til I got older. Uncle Nicky passed away, and [his was] the first funeral I went to when I was young, but my dad would still go see Aunt Mel to keep in touch.

Uncle Johnny got remarried. I don't remember his first wife, but his second wife had a child with him that was the same age as my daughter, so I would see them at my parents' house every now and then. But I've never ever seen my aunts at my parents' house. I don't know why, but I know my aunt Helen and my mom didn't like each other. And Aunt Yolanda, she seem to stay away and raise her daughters. I always felt dirty and poor around her, but she never treated me like that when we went over there. She was pretty, smart, shy and wasn't poor.

So bad stuff happened between my dad and me; it took a long time before I could talk to him again. After that, I came clean about how I felt and how I remembered some things. And I asked him: was he this way because of the way he grew up? And he would just nod his head. My dad only hit me once. I was ten maybe, and trust me, I deserved it! So it wasn't the beatings and stuff his dad did to him, so I needed to know what the hell happened to him to make him turn out that way.

So I sat him down, and I told him he owed me the truth. They say once you're abused, if you don't get help, you could become an abuser. Well, like I said, my dad didn't hit me, and I can't remember most of my childhood for some reason. Well, my dad was an abuser; he sexually abused and admitted it and went to jail for a couple days. Then he had to go to therapy, and our whole family knew what was going on. I am not saying who or how many, but I will say I can't remember. I just have little flashbacks, but I still am not sure if it was by him. His sisters and brothers never knew secrets again.

We all moved on with our lives and tried hard to be a family, and all I thought I wanted was approval from my parents, but I now know, as I sit here and type, that I want answers.

Years went by, and my dad had surgery on his neck to open some of the clogged arteries that made him have bad headaches. My dad wasn't the healthiest man alive. He was a truck driver all his life and smoked like three to four packs of cigarettes a day. Drank coffee all day long and had high blood pressure, stroke—many issues. Well when they opened the arteries, he got a brain aneurysm, really not sure if he had it before, but he was going to get it operated on. So when we came down from upstate—where my husband and I lived with our kids—to see him before the next surgery on his brain, I am glad we did. It was the first time I think I saw true love from my dad. He told me he was scared, but the headaches were too bad, and he couldn't handle it and the medicine didn't help. So we chatted, and he opened up all on his own. He was giving me some answers without me asking. I was shocked. And my mom was right there as he was telling me. I have heard rumors when I was younger that my mom hated Aunt Helen because Aunt Helen wanted to be my dad's wife. Maybe that is where he learned his abuse. But I never believed. My family is full of storytellers, but some are half true. Aunt Helen was a classy lady, and her nose was always in the air. I thought she didn't get along with anyone. For some reason, I don't know why, she didn't even talk to her sister since as long as I knew them 'til a couple months before Uncle Johnny passed away in the summer of 2010. I saw them both at the funeral.

He told me all my digging for the truth about the family secret was scary to him but was happy that someday it would come out by me. He told me what he thought and told me if it was true, I could never prove it. So I asked again who got paid off at the trial. He said, "Who didn't?" I knew that since after the trial my grandmother lived, I think eight years longer, and the farm was sold to S. Kliens, a department store, and I have no idea what happen to all the money, but I do know Aunt Helen and her husband John Guanti lived very, very well.

My dad said he believes the whole murder was over money, and it was planned. He told me a story—now I don't know if it is true, but it sure sounds like it is. He said the beatings and all the abuse they talked about was real, they were not lying at all about one thing on that. But he had overheard that it was planned. He said that much he did know. He also said they lived the high life, and as a young guy with a shiny new car, he got many dates. He said some beatings, in a way, were deserved, as he and his brothers would get out of line—"wild," as he called it. He said that is why he had to join the army, to learn to behave and be a man. So was my grandfather mean or just being a father the best that he knew how in those times?

The story I was told, true or not, is that Uncle John Guanti was married to Aunt Helen and they had planned a way to get rid of the nasty mean old man, my grandfather, Mr. Bejamin D'Amore. So for the plan to work, the mastermind of it, Aunt Helen, had to get out of the picture. So she divorced my Uncle John and moved away and remarried to keep things real and keep herself safe and not a suspect. They were smart and had my Uncle Nicholas and Johnny so upset about my grandfather by telling them every little thing and even lies, getting them more and more enraged. Uncle John Guanti stayed and lived with my grandparents and reported my aunt Helen missing. They even had my grandmother more worried and in more fear of my grandfather than she already had been all the years before.

The beatings happened, but her sons were not living there anymore, so things had to be a little easier—or maybe not. They convinced my uncles that it had to stop and called them every time something was happening so they would get more and more angry. I heard they even did things to make my grandfather angry. So they sat down and talked about killing their father. I don't think the night that it happened was supposed to be that night, but it just seemed like the timing was right. They called my uncles over right after my grandparents had a fight and my grandfather had left and my grandmother was upset, so the ball was in motion. They were cheered on in a way that their anger got the best of them, so they decided to get the guns and show my grandfather a lesson. Aunt Helen was chatting in their ears about being men and saving their mother. So they waited and waited and got more mad, thinking it was time to stop all this madness. So when my grandfather got home, both my uncles were outside and shot their guns at him and killed him.

After the court was over, my ex-uncle John Guanti, who was the man who picked them all up at the courthouse and even posed in pictures, was back in charge of their lives, a father figure. My aunt divorced my uncle John Bolenski and remarried Uncle John Guanti. My father said that his two sisters didn't talk because of the money, and my aunt Helen felt she did the work, she wanted the money. And her now husband, John Guanti, was my grandfather's partner and got the business. My aunt Yolanda didn't know about the plan, and when she found out, she wanted nothing to do with Aunt Helen. My father was away on base with the army and was called home because of the murder. But he said he learned of all this because my uncle Johnny couldn't deal with what he had done and needed to tell someone.

So this is what I was told, true or not, but it makes some sense of it all. I didn't wish to upset anyone that I care about, but the ones I do care about are all passed away, so that is why I am writing this. My aunt Helen and her husband, Uncle John, are still alive. They have lived with this most of their lives, and it doesn't seem to bother them, so why would my words, since they are only my words.

My dad passed away from the brain surgery he had in September 1995 and never woke up and passed in December 1995. I remember Aunt Helen sitting there, and everyone talked to her, and I asked who she was because she was being snotty to my mom. My sister said it's Aunt Helen, but you might know her as Aunt Nellie. I didn't recognize her. That was the first time I ever heard her called that. She was a mean woman at that time. She made my mom—I have no idea what hold she had on my mom—take pictures at my dad's funeral because she wasn't going because my mom was having him cremated. And I wouldn't have known this if I didn't find the pictures of him in his coffin that my mom was putting in an envelope to send to Aunt Helen. And that was the day that I started to believe that maybe I was right about Aunt Helen abusing my father. But I still, to this day, have no idea what the deal is with her and my mom.

I feel if I tell this story, since it has been with me for so long, that maybe the people I love and lost can rest in peace. And maybe I can break this chain of abuse that runs in our family. Let us learn to love and care about each other without demands or pain. And maybe my grandfather was a bad man, but I think I would rather have seen him do time in jail than get part of his head blown away.

There is one chain I broke in my family, and that was to be there for my children and to love them always. I know I wasn't the best—I really didn't have any role models—but I did the best I could, and they always knew I was there for them. My husband, Jeff, and my children showed me what love was, and I want to thank them for that. My children and husband are my world, and now that it is growing with grandbabies, I want them to have great memories of their family, which starts with me and them.

Now that this secret is coming out, I don't feel lost anymore. I know who I am and what a messed up family I came from. I don't fear what they have to say or the way they look at me. Aunt Helen, I hope you are happy with the fights and pain you have caused my mother. And I believe my mother, even though she would say it under her breath, that you and only you caused and inflicted pain on my father when he was a young man. Somehow you had power over the family. Could it be because you took most of what was theirs, including their father?

One question I have for you Aunt Nellie—or Aunt Helen or whatever your name is these days—who do you hold power over now? I can tell you it is *not* my mom or dad and definitely *not* me!

I want my parents to know I love them, even if our lives had so much to deal with. I do believe my mom was depressed for years when I was young and that is why she wasn't there for me as a young child. And I do believe my father's cheating was a big part of it. Or was it his problem that he was trying to deal with because of what had happened to him? Still no excuses, but it is a shame that they didn't get help. And why did they stay together? Family secrets do so much harm for years to old family members and new ones. I won't hide who I am to my kids or my husband or, most of all, to myself. I hereby announce that the D'Amore secret holds nothing over me anymore. The only thing I wonder is: was my grandfather this bad man since none of you children called the police, saw a doctor or broke a bone, or was he caught up in someone's greed for the money? That money could have gone to all his children to build a life that they had a right to since their father had worked so hard for it.

But if the story is true about my aunt Helen, then I don't even want to ask her why she needed the money so bad. The money is tainted now, and you had to live with that. I hope you and your husband felt some remorse. You two are the family's dirty secret, as I see it. And these are my words, with every little piece I could put together from my past: it was you.

And yet, you would have my dad over like you cared about him. If you cared, you should have made sure he went back in the army after the murder trial was over so he could have become what he wanted. I still don't get why he wasn't sent back. But I guess it was better to keep someone you controlled close to you, but it seems you controlled all your brothers. When I saw you at Uncle Johnny's funeral, we had this talk. I leaned to you and said, "I know what you did to my father, and I have a good idea what you did to your own father."

And all you could say is, "Why doesn't my brother have a headstone at his grave? Even Aunt Yolanda said the same."

I said, "Why do you care? You didn't even come to his funereal."

Someday, we will have a headstone at my mother and father's grave since they are buried together as man and wife. But I can't do anything because it is my sister's plot where my mother and father are buried. And I'll make sure my sister doesn't move them from graveyard to graveyard like you did with your parents. Why did you do that?

The big D'Amore plot with a great big headstone with "Guanti, D'Amore" on one headstone, are you sure you want to rest in peace with that on there?

Maybe this seems like an attack, and maybe it is. Or maybe it is just a way of making you feel the way you made me feel my whole life. I'm not a dirty little girl, and I don't think I really ever was. I was just left behind by people who should have loved and guided me. I can say that I learned from my mistakes and try to do my best in my life as I go.

I know families have things they hide from their children, like worrying about paying bills or fights that parents have or even worse things, but I never thought my family secret would be that I have murderers in my family and they got away with it.

I love you, Mom and Dad, and someday we will meet again with no shame, no heartaches, just love and peace. And, Dad, I kept my promise.

Dawn Anita D'Amore Yankanich

2
CROSSING OVER TO AMERICA

Hundreds of millions of people, either as individuals or in family groups, have traveled the long and not-too-safe journey across the Atlantic Ocean to chase the American dream. Poles, Irish, Italians, Germans, Quakers and citizens from almost every nation boarded steamships in hope of landing in this country just to make a better life for themselves.

They came for different reasons. In the 1600s, they came to escape the iron hand of religious intolerance, to escape natural disasters like famine and for work. No matter what their motivation, these immigrants saw America as a shining light, a country that would lift them from the doldrums of existence in their native lands and, in doing so, bring hope, success and well-being.

Immigrants bought passage on all type of ships, usually at the lowest possible class rate, known as steerage, where they were stuffed together—men, women and children—in conditions that would be beyond tolerance to modern-day individuals. The environment was hot, cramped and downright unbearable. Yet still they came and came and came.

Some made it; some did not. Illness may have taken some mid-voyage; accidents surely took a large number before they ever reached their destination. Since these people were relegated to the least desirable levels of the ships, it was a death sentence should there be any type of major accident. In the most infamous shipping disaster of all time, the sinking of the RMS *Titanic*, of the 708 passengers in steerage (White Star Line, the owners of the ship, officially referred to steerage as "third class"), 528 were lost to the sea. By far, it was the highest loss of life of any class of passenger

The D'Amores' American dream. *By Sally Klann.*

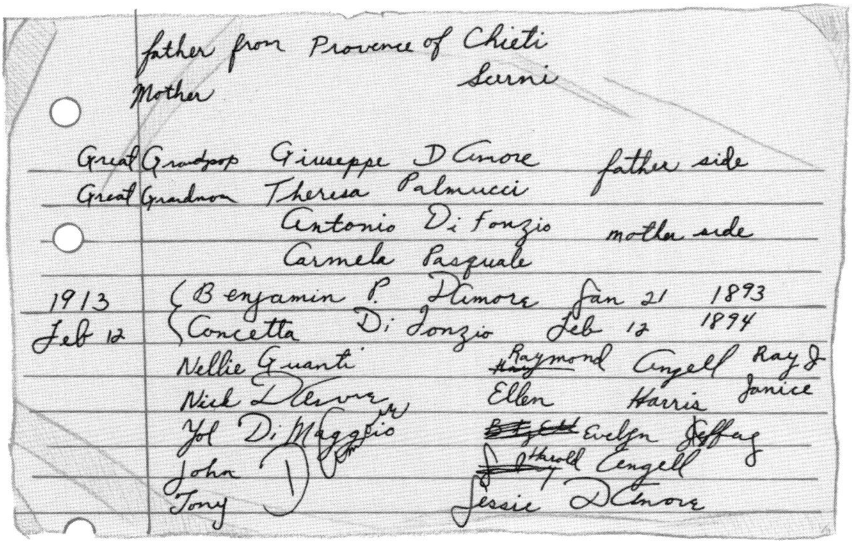
father from Province of Chieti
Mother Scerni
Great Grandpop Giuseppe D'Amore father side
Great Grandmom Theresa Palmucci
Antonio Di Fonzio mother side
Carmela Pasquale
1913 { Benjamin P. D'Amore Jan 21 1893
Feb 12 { Concetta Di Fonzio Feb 12 1894
Nellie Guanti Raymond Angell Ray J
Nick D'Amore Ellen Harris Janice
Yol DiMaggio Evelyn
John Angell
Tony Jessie D'Amore

Handwritten D'Amore genealogy. *By Sally Klann.*

that evening. Numerous accounts of the accident report that there was no attempt to rescue the passengers in steerage.

If an immigrant did safely reach the shores of America, it was still no bed of roses. Most were treated badly at the point of entry. Their names may have been changed by immigration officials who just did not understand the broken English some people spoke; they were made to live in tenements in sweltering cities and work for subsistence wages. On top of all these hardships, they were often the target of discrimination and crime. Yet still they came. And crossing over to America, with their fellow Italian countrymen and countrywomen, were Penfilo D'Amore and his wife, Concetta.

Scerni is an Italian town of about 3,400 residents, located in the Province of Chieti in Abruzzo, Italy. It is on the back of the Italian boot, the side of Italy that borders the Adriatic Sea, almost halfway between Pescara to the north and Termoli to the south. Scerni is an ancient city dating back to 1324. Its original inhabitants were Abruzzese shepherds who used it as a way station during the twice-yearly sheep drives going to and returning from Apuila. Research of modern-day Scerni shows it is located in a fertile farming area with access to both the coastline and mountain areas. It is interesting that the patron saint of the town of Scerni is, in fact, St. Panfilo, the namesake of Panfilo D'Amore, Benjamin's original name.

Scerni was, apparently, the family home of Concetta. While, at present, there is no available official documents memorializing the birth of Panfilo, a *Certificato Di Nascita* (certificate of birth) shows that Concetta Di Fonzo was born in Scerni on February 12, 1894, and, according to a *Certicato Di Matrimonis* (certificate of marriage), was wed to Panfilo D'Amore on February 11, 1912. According to an e-mail sent to the author by Emido Spinogatti, administrator of the website www.AbruzzoGenealogy.com, it is very possible that Panfilo did not actually come from Scerni. Spinogatti wrote, "The surname [D'Amore] seems not typical of Scerni, so probably the D'Amore family came from other places, possibly the L'Aquila province in Abruzzo."[3]

The next documented mention of Panfilo D'Amore shows up on "List or Manifest of Alien Passengers for the United States," dated March 13, 1913. Panfilo's name appears as having booked passage on the SS *America*, which departed from the Italian city of Naples. There is no point of entry noted, and Concetta's name does not appear anywhere on the manifest.

A registration card (possibly used to keep track of the location of aliens) dated June 5, 1917, shows Panfilo living at 310 County Line Road in Ardmore, Pennsylvania. It describes him as short, of medium build, with brown eyes and black hair and lists his occupation as "labor."

The first appearance of a family related to Panfilo shows up on an untitled document issued by the District Court of the Eastern District of

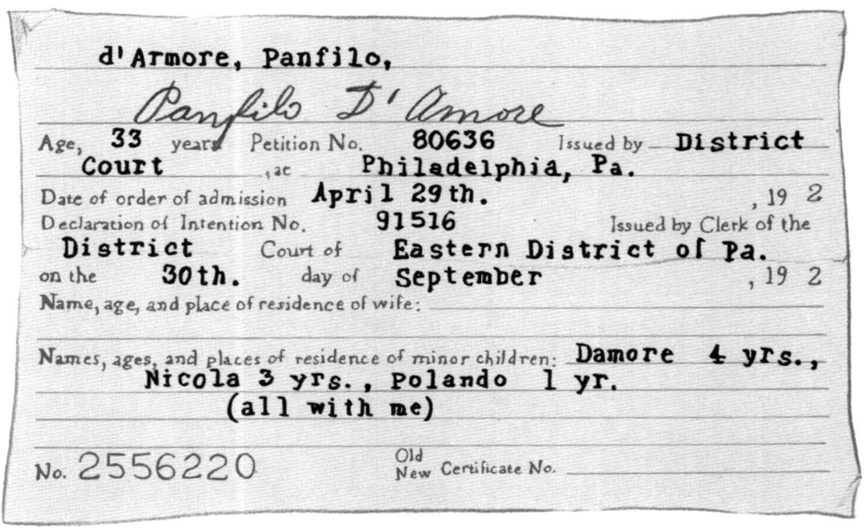
d'Armore, Panfilo,
Panfilo D'Amore
Age, 33 years Petition No. 80636 Issued by District Court, at Philadelphia, Pa.
Date of order of admission April 29th., 19 2
Declaration of Intention No. 91516 Issued by Clerk of the District Court of Eastern District of Pa.
on the 30th. day of September, 19 2
Name, age, and place of residence of wife:
Names, ages, and places of residence of minor children: Damore 4 yrs., Nicola 3 yrs., Polando 1 yr.
(all with me)
No. 2556220 Old New Certificate No.

Benjamin's alien registration card. *By Sally Klann.*

Pennsylvania. It shows D'Amore as petitioner 80636 and is dated April 29, 192? (the last number in the year is cut off). While Concetta's name does not appear, the names of two D'Amore children are noted, Nicola, three years old, and Polando, one year old. The latter is most likely a misspelling of D'Amore's daughter Yolanda.

Finally, in the United States census dated April 9, 1930, the names of Panfilo, Concetta and their five children are recorded. The location of the D'Amore residence is in the thirty-fourth ward, block 444 in Philadelphia, Pennsylvania. (According to a 1930 map of Philadelphia, the thirty-fourth ward is in West Philadelphia and borders Delaware County to the south and Montgomery County to the north. Block 444 is bordered by Lansdown Avenue to the north, North Sixty-second Street to the east, Haverford Avenue to the south and North Sixty-fourth Street to the west.)

While there is really no information on the movement of the D'Amore family after 1930, a passenger list for an unnamed ship records an individual named Panfilo D'Amore as having left Buenos Aires, Argentina, on July 23, 1948, and having arrived in New York City on August 9 of the same year. There is no doubt that this is Panfilo since the address listed on the document is RD 1, Sproul–State Road, Media, Pennsylvania, the exact location of the State Road Nursery owned by D'Amore. There is no information about why D'Amore was in Argentina or that any member of his family was with him. It is noted on the document that D'Amore was traveling first class.

D'Amore's travel to Argentina is curious. The year 1948 was really at the very beginnings of the era of Juan Peron. The dictator had taken office after being elected in February 1946. Peron's strong-arm regime did little to make Argentina an attractive destination for tourists, since the economy suffered badly. Why then, would D'Amore, a nursery owner from Marple Township, Pennsylvania, visit Argentina? There does not seem to be any evidence that Argentina was, in any way, a producer or exporter of products that could be used to boost inventory in the nursery business.

Of course, the primary reason, after tourism, that people visit other countries is to find or visit with relatives. Research shows that Argentina has a significant population of citizens with some connection to Italy through immigration. It is possible that D'Amore was there to look up long-lost relatives. If that is so, then why did he go alone?

With little information to go on, it can be assumed that once Panfilo (now known to the community as Benjamin) moved his family to Marple Township, they—like millions of immigrants before them—assimilated into the American way of life. They ran a business, raised a family and were productive members of the community. Somehow, somewhere, something went wrong in the D'Amore family. Benjamin became an abuser of his wife and children. Why? Who knows. It is fair to say that if he was an abuser in America, then he must have been an abuser in Italy. Whether he was or not, the entire D'Amore family's picture of a great life in America on a nursery in Marple Township was shattered to pieces by the blasts from two guns.

3
A PAIR OF DIRTY SOCKS

On November 20, 1949, the chain of events that led to the gunning down of Benjamin D'Amore by his two sons was supposed to have started over a pair of dirty socks. The sons would say that the sock incident was just the straw that broke the camel's back as far as they were concerned. It was the culmination of years of abuse, and they both believed that it was time to put an end to the fear and pain that they and their mother had endured at the hands of Benjamin D'Amore. Why did he want to wear a specific pair of socks? Maybe they were his favorite, or maybe he just thought that they went nicely his outfit. Nobody really knows, but what is known is that this particular pair of socks was not available because they were dirty.

According to the boys' mother, this sent D'Amore into a fit of rage and resulted in a solid beating as punishment for not having the socks clean and ready to wear. Describing the abuse that day for an article in the *Philadelphia Evening Bulletin*, D'Amore's son-in-law John Guanti said, "He gave her quite a going over."

The house in which the "going over" was given is gone now. So is the nursery that Benjamin D'Amore owned. The land is now occupied by a strip shopping center that includes the usual specialty and big-box stores. Two limited access highways, U.S. Route 1 and Interstate 476, cut through what was the property. There is no sign of the area ever having been a crime scene. If the people who visit the retail stores were asked about the murder, it is a good bet that none would have heard about it or, for that matter, had any interest in it.

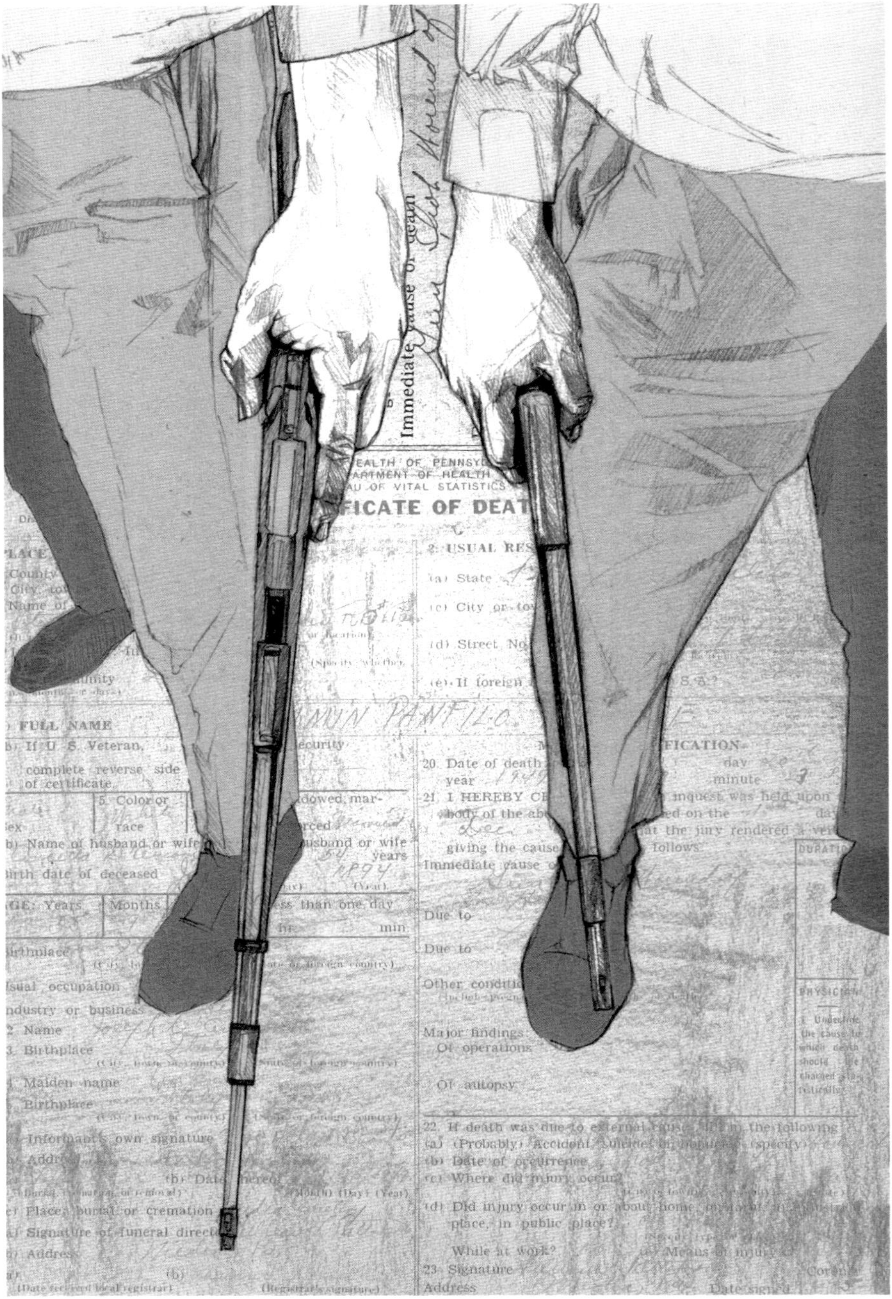

The D'Amore brothers were armed with a deer rifle and a shotgun. *By Sally Klann.*

The D'Amore murder house. *By Sally Klann.*

The only view of the murder scene, at least of the house, comes from a newspaper photo printed in a local Delaware County paper. It seems to be a typical Pennsylvania farmhouse. The Colonial-type architecture dotted southeastern Pennsylvania, but few remain entirely standing today. From time to time, the remains of this type of house—usually one or two stone walls or a square stone foundation—are visible from a roadway when the fall season starts to strip the leaves from the trees.

From the photo and the illustration that accompanies this story, the house was two and a half stories. Typically, the first floor had a kitchen, dining room and living area; the second story held bedrooms; and the third story was taken up by a small attic used for storage. Most of the time, these houses had basements or cellars that, in colonial times, were used for storage of vegetables and other perishable items.

The exterior walls were almost always constructed of stone cut from local quarries or found in the neighboring forest or creek side. The exterior walls were normally white from paint or whitewash, which was used as a sealer to protect the mortar from the wear of rain and snow.

Sometimes there were outbuildings, root houses and other small structures used to store meat, grain or wood. Garages, if they existed, were probably built by later owners and were usually made of wood.

Inside, the rooms may have been small compared to today's construction. Floors were made of wood cut from local trees, and originally, heat was generated from fireplaces in various rooms.

These houses were originally homesteads, and because Delaware County was first made up of large land-grant properties, there was often some distance between neighbors, which made it very easy for activities, both good and bad, to go on unnoticed. Even though an aerial view of the property, dated 1953, shows some residential development in the area, it is possible that the sounds of physical abuse went unnoticed within the thick stone walls of a house set deep on a wooded property. This may very well be what took place in the D'Amore family home. The sounds of a fist hitting a face or the screams of children locked in a basement would be heard only by the abuser and the abused.

It is not hard to both understand and empathize with the D'Amore family if the motive for the murder was fear of abuse. They lived in an isolated house, always waiting for an abusive father to return home from work, fearing a beating or, at best, a stint in the basement prison in handcuffs. Anyone in that position might very well want the abuser out of the way and plan, from childhood, to find a method to rid the family of the problem. After all, during the trial, both brothers said that they had been "figuring" ever since they were boys that someday they might have to kill their father. Self-protection and the need to protect other family members is a strong emotional drive; it's fight or flight at its most basic level. It may very well be that the D'Amore brothers had no alternative but to fight to save themselves and their mother. What took place on the day of the dirty socks may have been inevitable. Of course, it all may have been a smokescreen—elaborate street theater fueled by greed. For sure, greed can be a much stronger motive than fear.

November 21, 1949, was a Monday. According to historical weather information, the temperature hovered around forty-six degrees Fahrenheit. The winter had seen little snow, so the ground around the D'Amore home would have been free of any cover. Civil twilight was recorded at 5:11 p.m. The moon was in a waxing crescent phase with only 3 percent illumination. The area would have been dark and cast in shadow from any artificial lighting that had been installed between the home and the garage.

The headlights of Benjamin D'Amore's new car would have increased the illumination and put D'Amore himself directly in it as he got out of the vehicle, passed in front of it and moved toward the garage. He would have been an almost perfect target.

As with many modern-day crimes, information on the time leading up to the event is lacking. With the exception of one person, D'Amore's daughter Helen, everybody else involved that day is dead. To date, Helen has not spoken to any other member of the family about the crime for reasons only she knows.

Even the facts of that day became confusing because, during the sons' trial, certain inconsistencies surfaced during testimony. Of course, inconsistencies are not that unusual during testimony, either due to the time between the actual crime and the start of the trial or simply because a good defense attorney can introduce issues that he or she thinks are beneficial to the accused and will create reasonable doubt. The only fact that seems to be the same throughout the murder and trial is that the D'Amore boys admitted to killing their father and stuck to that story until the trial ended.

What appears to be fact is that, during the day of the murder, several individuals were in the D'Amore residence. Concetta D'Amore, the boys' mother, was there, as was John Guanti, Helen's husband and Benjamin's partner in the nursery business. Guanti, who died in 2013, is a somewhat shadowy figure in the D'Amore family story. He was married to Helen for a time, then Helen divorced John, only to marry a second John, this one with the last name of Bolenski. Helen subsequently divorced Bolenski and remarried John Guanti. They remained married until his death. The third D'Amore son, Anthony, was away at army boot camp and was not involved with the shooting.

It also seems that Guanti was the first person to tell the sons that their father had beat their mother that night. Guanti also told the boys that the motive for the beating was the father's desire for a specific pair of socks that Concetta had not yet washed. Of course, if Guanti witnessed the actual beating, why did he not make an attempt to stop it? During testimony at the trial, at least one person employed by D'Amore said that he witnessed Benjamin physically abuse the family members and did nothing to stop him.

On the day of the crime, November 21, 1949, the two brothers happened to stop over at the family residence around 6:00 p.m. in order to borrow an electric fan. At this point, John Guanti told them about the beating of their mother. Since their father had left the property for some reason, the boys had

Concetta, John, Nick and Helen. *By Sally Klann.*

no way of finding out the father's side of the story and, apparently, took Guanti at his word. Guanti's story and what appeared to be bruises on their mother drove the brothers into a rage, and the plan to murder their father took form.

John, twenty-two at the time, sent his brother Nicholas, twenty-six, to the former's home around Forty-minth Street and Parkside Avenue in Philadelphia. Nicholas was told to retrieve John's deer rifle and bring it back to the D'Amore homestead even though the boys knew that their father kept a shotgun at the house. According MapQuest, the trip from the nursery on State and Sproul Roads to the home in Philadelphia would be about twenty to twenty-six miles and should have taken around sixty minutes round trip. When Nicholas returned to Marple Township with the second weapon, Benjamin D'Amore had not yet returned home. If the mileage and travel time are near correct and if Nicholas had left Marple around 7:30 p.m., he would have been back in Marple anytime between 9:30 and 10:00 p.m. What happened at the D'Amore home between the time Nicholas returned and their father got back is really not known. Those in the house must have talked about the plan of the upcoming murder. It would have been impossible for the other family members to not realize what was about to happen when the two brothers were armed with a deer rifle and a shotgun. One of the unanswered questions of that evening is why Helen, John and Concetta didn't try to talk the boys out of executing their father. Certainly, under any legal definition, if Helen, John or Concetta concurred with the boy's plan, they had entered into a criminal conspiracy. This is regardless of the fact that the two boys confessed to both the police and the jury that they had committed the murder. The other three conspirators could still have been charged. Why they were not charged remains unanswered.

At about 11:00 p.m., Benjamin's car could be heard coming up the driveway. He intended to put the vehicle in the garage, which, according to the illustration, was at the rear of the house. When D'Amore got out of the car, crossed in front of it and headed toward the garage, the boys opened up on him. (At this point, testimony is inconsistent. It is not clear whether the boys were already outside of the house or were waiting inside and came out when their father got out of his car.)

Nicholas may have fired first and missed. He reloaded and fired a second time. John's gun went off just once. (There was more inconsistency during the testimony—one of the brothers said that his gun just went off, not that he had fired it intentionally.) The father, his head blown almost completely off, fell in front of his car. He was probably dead before his body hit the ground. Sometime shortly after, John Guanti called both the Marple Township and Springfield Township police departments and reported the crime.

There were two ear witnesses to the shooting. One was Harry Meyers—who just happened to be a consulting criminologist and a past Pennsylvania State Police Academy instructor—lived about three hundred feet from the D'Amore homestead. Meyers was doing some paperwork in his home when he heard shots. He said that he saw the two D'Amore brothers outside and asked them what and happened. One of the boys told Meyers that everything was OK, and Meyers took the brother at his word. He went back into his house and resumed his work. The arrival of the police left Meyers with the impression that everything was definitely not OK.

The other witness was Ted Muehlmatt. In a personal interview with him, which took place on Monday, April 13, 2015, Muehlmatt said that he and his family, who lived close to the D'Amore nursery, were gathered in their home when they heard shots. Muehlmatt went on to say that the various family members agreed that they all had heard something that sounded like gunfire. Muehlmatt, recalling an event that took place sixty-five years in the past, said that the shots were heard sometime between 11:00 p.m. and midnight. This timeframe fits with the fact that Benjamin was murdered sometime around 11:30 p.m. (Ernest Muehlmatt, Ted's father, went on to appear as a witness for the defense in the D'Amore trial and corroborated, by testimony, the facts of abuse that were entered into evidence.)

When two officers from Springfield and the Marple Township police chief arrived, the two boys gave up their weapons and confessed that they had murdered their father. Both brothers were taken to the police station in Springfield and then transferred to the Delaware County Courthouse in Media, where further questioning followed. Benjamin's car was taken to a

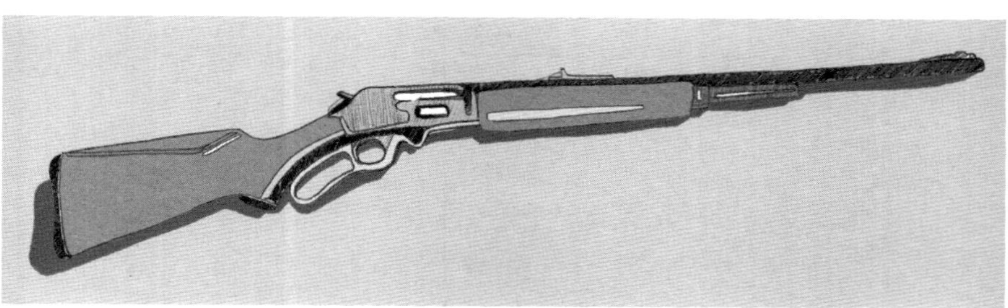

A deer rifle similar to one used in the murder. *By Sally Klann.*

Anthony with Benjamin's car several days after the murder. *By Sally Klann.*

local service garage but returned to the D'Amores shortly afterward. The next day, at a preliminary hearing before the Marple Township magistrate, the two brothers were formally charged with the murder of their father, Benjamin D'Amore. Bail was denied.

4
MOTIVE

Motive is the reason people do things. It can be as simple as the reason that an obese individual decides to lose weight—because it will make him healthier and prolong his life. In a legal sense, motive is important, but not as important as most people think.

The prosecution does not have to prove motive in order to present a case. The prosecution does not even have to bring up motive, but most people who watch police procedurals on TV, where motive is a large part of the plot, accept the fact that motive is important. There are some cases where the prosecution finds motive invaluable in order to get a conviction, such as a wife murdering her husband after finding out he is having an affair. The prosecutor will insert motive, jealousy and revenge into the case in order to lay groundwork for the jury, urging them toward a guilty verdict.

On the other hand, the prosecution may want to stay away from too much emphasis on motive because it could hinder the case and lead to a sympathetic jury coming out on the side of the defendant with an acquittal or, worse, a hung jury. Sympathy for the defendant can overshadow the standard of "beyond a reasonable doubt" and end in a prosecutorial embarrassment when the defendant charged with a serious crime walks out of the courthouse a free person.

People, sometimes half in jest, will say that neither guilty verdicts nor acquittal have anything to do with the truth, and this may very well be true because if a good defense lawyer can use motive to garner sympathy for the defendant, acquittal may very well be the outcome of the trial. The D'Amore

Caught in the headlights. *By Sally Klann.*

murder case may have been a perfect example. Aided by a brilliant move on the part of defense attorney, and what has been a highly questionable judgment by the prosecutor, motive played a major part in the case. In fact, the decision of the jury may very well have turned on it.

In the case of the D'Amore murder, the motive was abuse. Actually, it was the collective incidents of abuse over the years that triggered the shooting. In his book *The Meaning of Anxiety*, Revised Edition, Rollo May said that "every human being has a 'threshold' beyond which additional stress makes the situation catastrophic."[4] In an e-mail to the author from Dr. Shana Maier, PhD, director of the masters in criminal justice program at Widener University in Chester, Pennsylvania, and expert in intimate partner abuse, agreed, saying, "If they [the D'Amore brothers] lived a life where they witnessed domestic violence all the time, then violence would have been normalized for them. They may have seen the killing of their father differently than someone who has not witnessed violence on a regular basis."[5]

So the question remains: was the alleged abuse suffered by the entire family at the hands of the father enough to throw the brothers into what psychiatric expert testimony termed a "catathymic crises," which triggered "certain inner perceptions…associated with a past experience [that] produced…fear of punishment or actual punishment"?[6] Or was the alleged abuse just a good excuse to do away with the father for financial gain?

The fact that abuse played a big part in the lives of the D'Amores remains conjecture due to one important fact: family abuse was not that big a deal. Of course, this attitude was based on women's place in society. In both the seventeenth and eighteenth centuries—and in the United States, having just come through World War II—the culture was still highly patriarchal. It was a man's world, and women were expected to toe the line when it came to their place.

In a March 2015 phone conversation with the author, Dr. Maier discussed this issue in some detail, particularly when it came to family abuse. According to Dr. Maier, when a women was being abused by her spouse, she had no real protection, socially or legally. In fact, any family member—be it wife, sons or daughters—was out in the cold when it came to expecting any outside protection from an abusive spouse or father. Dr. Maier emphasized that there were very few shelters or governmental resources that families or women could go to if they were in fear of sexual, physical or mental abuse. Abuse was "considered a private matter," in the words of Dr. Maier.

Law enforcement didn't get involved to any extent (except in a case of abuse that led to murder). As a matter of fact, calls to police for abuse, whether they were made by a member of the family or by an outsider, were handled much like a modern-day violation of a local nuisance ordinance. The screams of a child or wife being beaten, according to Dr. Maier, was typically "handled as any everyday noise complaint."

In fact, Dr. Maier said that things would not get much better for the abused until almost twenty years after the D'Amore murder, when the women's movement started up; protective legislation was passed, including the first battered woman's shelter in the early 1970s; and mandatory arrest laws went into effect in many jurisdictions in the mid-1980s.

It is very likely then, with the era's laissez-faire attitude concerning women and children, that the wife, sons and daughters of Benjamin D'Amore suffered greatly at his hands. However, was this abuse to the extent that the only way out of the conflict was murder?

Past studies have shown that abuse in families is hereditary, not in the same sense as blue eyes or red hair, but in the sense that it is a learned activity, passed down from parents to children who become parents and pass it on to their children. It is environmentally heredity. According to Dr. Maiers, the proper name for this is the "intergenerational cycle of abuse." Dawn D'Amore said that she was locked in the basement by her father, the same type of punishment that the two brothers suffered at the hands of their father, the murder victim.

It is true that many families go through all types of abuse, but those acts do not necessarily end in patricide as they did with the D'Amores. It all comes down, according to Rollo May, to two emotions: anxiety and fear. He said:

> *In fear, we are aware of ourselves as well as the object, and we can orient ourselves spatially with reference to the thing we fear. In anxiety…your efforts…generally amount to frantic behavior…* [Further] *an organism is thrown into a catastrophic condition when it cannot cope with the demands of its environment and therefore feels a threat to its existence or to values essential to that existence.*[7]

While it is obvious to all of us that abuse can create an environment of fear and anxiety, if we put the murder of Benjamin D'Amore into the context of the day of the crime, there is a good argument to be made that neither son was in a position to fear his father since when they arrived at the home, he was not there. They had more than ample time to, in the words of Rollo May, orient themselves spatially with reference to the thing they feared: their father. In this case, spatial orientation meant planning their father's murder. Of course, it is highly possible and very probable that they were filled with anxiety because of their mother's beating over a pair of dirty socks. It is, of course, only speculation that any anxiety already in place could have been heighted by the description of the beating that John Guanti gave to the brothers.

This anxiety must have led to intense anger. As Wade E. Pickerin pointed out in his book *The Psychology Book: From Sahmanism to Cutting Edge Neuroscience, 250 Years in the History of Psychology*, "Anger may lead to aggression if there are items (such as weapons) present when a person is most angry."[8]

On the night Benjamin D'Amore was executed, numerous issues aligned: past abuse, the alleged beating of Concetta D'Amore by her husband, the arrival of the two sons and the availability of at least one gun. Certainly, the confluence of these factors could lead to what the expert witnesses called a catathymic crises.

But one factor still remains suspect: time. The boys arrived around 6:00 p.m., and the father returned to the house sometime after 11:00 p.m. That's five hours! The theory of a catathymic crises becomes much more plausible if the scenario changes and puts the boys arriving while the father was in the house. Their mother sits beaten and bruised because of a pair of dirty socks. John Guanti tells the two boys about the beating. The boys, remembering all the past abuse laid upon them, become fearful. Fear turns into anger and anger into aggression. A gun is retrieved from the basement. In the minds of the boys, there is no other solution but to end this family nightmare. One of the sons raises the gun, aims at the father and pulls the trigger. The father falls to the floor, dead.

But that's not how it happened. The brothers waited for Benjamin to arrive home. In that time, one brother sent the other brother on a trip to Philadelphia to get a second gun, a shotgun much more powerful than the rifle that was already at the house. The other brother and the shotgun arrived, and still they waited and waited. They heard their father's car come up the drive; he parked it and got out. At this point, the sons saw their father silhouetted by the headlights. They snuck from the house, shouldered their weapons and shot. Benjamin's head took the full force of the blast from the guns. He slumped across the hood and slid down onto the ground in front of the car. The two sons had just successfully carried out the ultimate form of physical violence, keeping intact the intergenerational cycle of abuse.

And in the five-hour waiting time, they may have sat around a kitchen table discussing what was about to take place. While they had no idea what a catathymic crises was, they knew that stories of abuse, both mental and physical, would make a great motive and might even bring about a verdict of acquittal.

5

THE LADIES OF THE TIME

Was it difficult to be a woman in 1949? If women's position in the household had improved from the 1800s to the 1940s, then the entire outlook of women had also improved. If no improvement had been made during that period, then women had made no progress in how society viewed them. Men of the 1940s would probably say yes, women's position had improved; women would emphatically shout no, but only to one another and never in earshot of their husbands or bosses. And what about spousal abuse? Abuse—spousal in particular and family-wide in general—is, after all, the alleged motive that caused the D'Amore boys to blast their father. Did a woman's "place in the world" open her up to the likelihood of abuse? Abuse, in the form of a good beating now and then, would surely keep the "little lady" in her place. After all, wasn't it true that the ladies of the day were created to serve the men of the houses?

Anybody who watched TV knew that to be true. When Ward Cleaver came home each night after a long, hard, stressful day at the office, June, meticulously dressed in a nice demur frock, was always there to meet him at the door. The door at the Anderson home was always opened by the dutiful wife, Margaret, so her husband, Jim, could enter and start to destress from his hard day at work.

After all, father always knew best, and mother knew her place. Of course, it is pure supposition to think that if June or Margaret were not waiting at the door—if they were out somewhere with the rest of the girls enjoying a late lunch or early cocktail—Ward and Jim might be waiting to give their

Protecting Mom. *By Sally Klann.*

better halves, as John Guanti described it to the D'Amore brothers, "a good going over."

Accordingly, legend has it that in an edition of *Housekeeping Monthly*, an article entitled "The Good Wife's Guide" appeared. The article listed eighteen items that good wives needed to follow in order to keep their husbands happy. The last item was: "A good wife always knows her place."

Of course, *Housekeeping Monthly* did not do a follow-up article advising a husband what do to if his wife forgot "her place." From Benjamin D'Amore's point of view, his wife's place was to keep his socks clean in case he wanted a fresh pair. It appears that Benjamin D'Amore did not need any help from *Housekeeping Monthly* in order to put Concetta back "in her place."

Her name was Rosie the Riveter. She wasn't a real person; she was an image, an image of the American woman, strong, patriotic and quite able to do the men's jobs while they were off fighting to protect freedom during World War II. She was so popular that somebody wrote a song about her, and her face was posted in factories, stores and restaurants across the land. Rosie was the government's way of telling women that they were independent and pretty much able to do what they wanted to do—just because they were women and they were needed.

The late 1940s was a transitional time for women in society. Similar to a butterfly evolving from a caterpillar, women were moving away from their barefoot and pregnant, girl in her place, servant of her man roles to spreading their wings and flying on their own.

There are, however, two important arguments that would counter the concept of women in transition. First, there were many more Concetta D'Amores then there were Rosie the Riveters (Rosies were expected to fight back if their husbands laid a hand on them), and men, for the most part, still ruled the roost.

Another factor that Concetta may have had to deal with was cultural. The D'Amores were Italian to the point that both she and Benjamin were born in Italy. Their Italian heritage and culture would have been undiluted by the idea of Rosie the Riveter. Of course, many cultures are hierarchical when it comes to the family structure, and many cultures still see men as the primary force in the family. The overwhelming majority of these families live in domestic peace, unafraid that the husband or father might be an abusive tyrant.

So Concetta D'Amore, had a lot stacked against her to start with. She was a woman from a different culture, a wife existing in an era when nobody much cared about her rights or her welfare, locked in a marriage to a brutal husband. She was no Rosie the Riveter. She had a place in which to remain. That is, if the story of the D'Amore family and the monster that controlled them is to be believed.

6
THIS SHOULD HAVE BEEN A SLAM-DUNK

It was a case cops dream about and prosecutors delight in. On the other hand, it was a defense attorney's nightmare. Pennsylvania magisterial district justice and Widener University legal education professor Thomas Lacey called this type of murder case defense the "so what" defense. Approaching the jury, the defense attorney might say something like this, "Ladies and gentleman of the jury, my client's husband was found lying on the basement floor with numerous stab wounds from a large carving knife. My client, his wife, was found standing next to the body. She was covered with blood, holding a large carving knife and dripping with blood. So what?"

Cops usually deal in circumstance. They also proceed with an investigation using two methods, objective or subjective. In one, the cops have a pretty good idea who did it, so they build a case against that person using the available evidence; in the other, the cops have only a trail of evidence, so they follow that trail hoping it will lead them to the person who committed the crime. In most cases, the investigation ends in a highly circumstantial case.

When cops arrive on the scene of a murder, they usually (but not always) find a body or at least parts of a body. Sometimes, they find what they consider to be the murder weapon. If they are really lucky, they might find a witness or two still at the location of the crime. Even if the cops get really lucky with bodies and weapons and witnesses, the investigation can take a long time and may not end in a guilty verdict. But one thing the cops usually never find at the scene is the alleged murderer or murderers. Murderers, if found at the scene of the crime, seldom confess anyway.

The defendants. *By Sally Klann.*

The D'Amore brothers in custody. *By Sally Klann.*

That is why the D'Amore murder was so unique and unusual, as far as the cops were concerned. They arrived on the scene right after the murder was committed. They had the body of Benjamin D'Amore laying in the driveway with very little of his head left attached to the rest of him. And it only got better for the cops. They had witnesses on the scene: Helen; her husband, John; and Benjamin's wife, Concetta. But what really made the cops' day were that they had the murder weapons, the shotgun and the deer hunting rifle, and that the guns were still in the hands of the alleged murderers, the two D'Amore boys, who freely admitted to the cops that they had fired the shots that killed their old man. There was only one thing that would round out this case, and the cops had that, too. At least they thought they did.

What the cops didn't have might have been more important to solving the case than all the evidence. Evidence is fine, but it does not always lead to the correct conclusion. Witnesses are great to have, but sometimes they don't always see it right or, for that matter, tell it right. Then there were the two confessions. Confessions are the Holy Grails of police work, but they are not always complete, and every once in a while, they hide the real truth.

What the cops did not have was a complete understanding of the D'Amore family's background. They did not have a complete understanding of the possible involvement of the other three individuals at the house on the afternoon and night of the crime. They didn't think to look past the obvious to search for the obscure. They did not have a technically sophisticated crime scene analysis (CSI) unit. But what was the difference? They had the victim, weapons, witnesses, the shooters and confessions. What more could a cop want?

Mike Fahy knows a lot about crime scenes. He has visited quite a few of them in his thirty-two-year career on the job as a highly respected member of the Philadelphia, Pennsylvania Police Department. Mike started out as a patrol officer in Philly's seventeenth and eighteenth police districts. He worked in the Juvenile Division and retired from the department as a detective in the Major Crimes Division.

Mike said that it was, "easy to see how a small jurisdiction, without vast resources, would take the word of the two brothers and just file charges without much investigation."[9] In small communities, the cops know a lot of the citizens, and to Mike, the admissions were pretty straightforward.

In the present day, according to Mike, the crime scene investigation would have been much more thorough and intense. "All persons from the house would have been interrogated [and] checked as well for gunpowder residue [using] paraffin."[10] Ballistics evidence would have been tagged and bagged, photos would have been taken and the house, weapons and Benjamin's body would have been checked for fingerprints. Finally, Mike said, "the use of polygraph was common back in the '50s," therefore, the use of that technique should have been considered.[11]

With the two major factors—lack of modern CSI methods and up-front confessions by both boys—the cops felt that they had all they needed. The case was closed.

It would have been the same for the prosecution, in this case the district attorney's office of Delaware County, Pennsylvania. After the cops made the arrest, the brothers would have been taken to a local justice of the peace for arraignment. If there was enough evidence that they had committed the murder, they would have been bound over for trial; bail, if any, would have been set; and they would have been transported to the Delaware County Jail to await whatever came next. The cops would have turned the evidence over to the district attorney, and a lawyer from that office would take over the case.

The main entrance of the Delaware County Courthouse. *By Sally Klann.*

That's the way it went for the D'Amore brothers. Charged with murder in the first, with bail denied, they were to spend their first night in jail. The assistant district attorney started to plan the case, a case he knew he was going to win. His name was R. Paul Lessy.

7

GIRL POWER IN THE JURY BOX

A lot of things were different in the United States in 1950, one being how people got their news. There wasn't any Court TV, CNN, MSNBC or Fox News to bring national events directly into people's living rooms. Even if there were, only about 3.8 million homes across the county had any television sets to watch (compared with about 115 million in 2014). Local new was not really a big draw as far as TV went, and there weren't any all-news radio stations, à la KYW. The only way people got information on what was happening around them was through local newspapers. According to numbers from the Newspaper Association of America, in 1950, there were 1,772 daily newspapers in the United States, having a total circulation of 53,838,000 (morning and evening).

So it fell to the local Delaware County newspaper, the *Chester Times* (now the *Delaware County Daily Times*), and the two major Philadelphia dailies, the *Philadelphia Inquirer* and the *Philadelphia Bulletin*, to cover both the murder and the trial.

The first-degree murder trial of the two D'Amore brothers was called to order on Monday, January 2, 1950, by the Honorable William R. Toal. (The Toal name went on to become quite famous in Delaware County jurisprudence. To date, there have been three generations of Toals involved in the judicial system, and a building located on the grounds of the Delaware County Courthouse is named the Toal Building.) The next day, Tuesday, January 3, the *Chester Times* printed its first article on the trial proceedings.

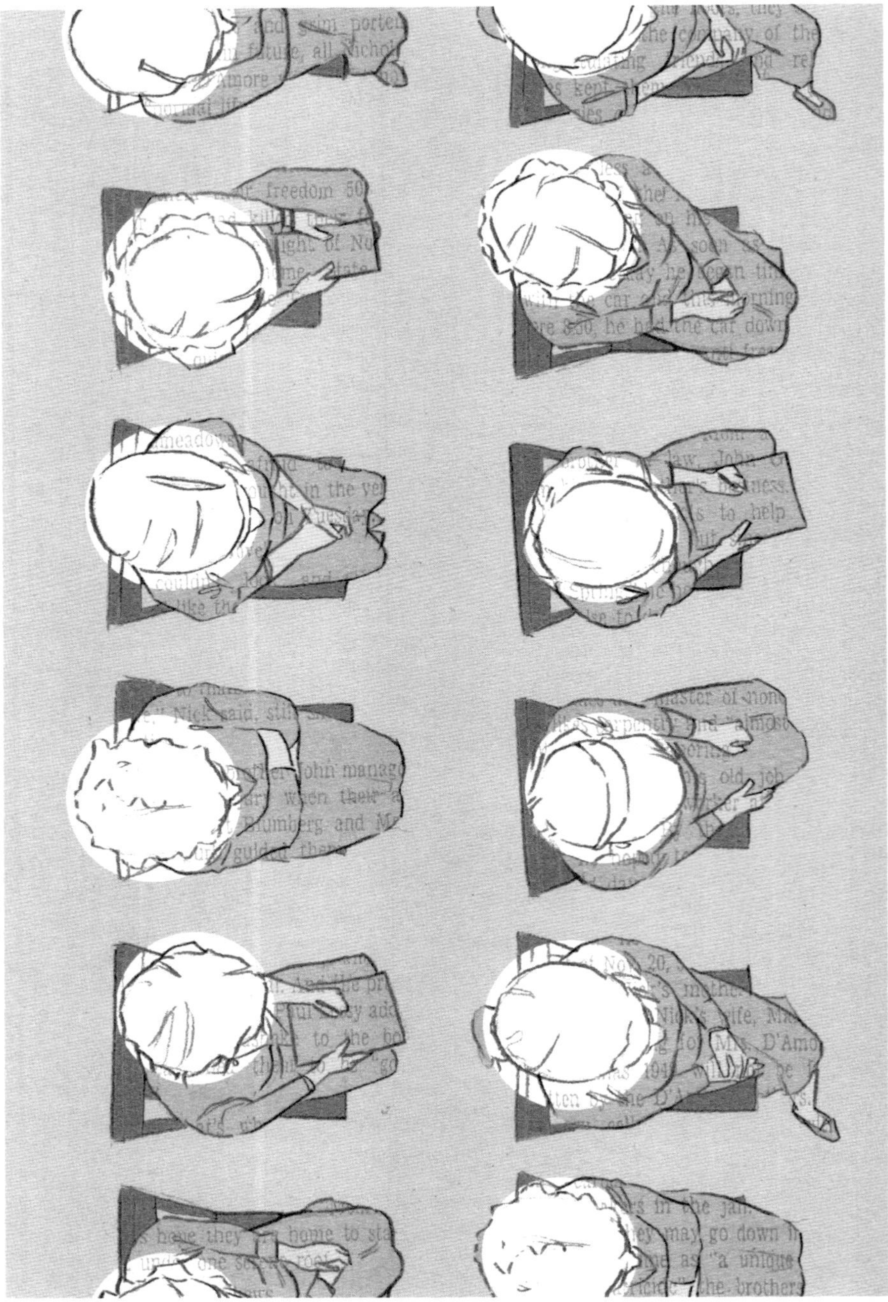

The ladies of the jury. *By Sally Klann.*

Day one, according to the newspaper, was taken up by *voir dire*. The American trial system is adversarial in nature, like a boxing match where two fighters throw punches at each other, all the while trying to fend off a major blow that might cause one to lose. In the case of the trial system, the two lawyers take the place of the fighters, and they dance around each other, attempting to score points with the members of the jury.

From the start, however, the prosecution, in agreement with the boys' defense attorney, made several unusual decisions when it came to the way the trial went forward. These decisions seemed even more unusual since, according to an unsigned article in the January 3, 1950 edition of the *Philadelphia Evening Bulletin*, "Assistant District Attorney R. Paul Lessy indicated by his questioning of prospective jurors that he would seek the death penalty."[12] (In another unsigned article from the same paper in a January 4 edition, it said that while "Lessy demanded that the brothers be found guilty of the murder, he said nothing about asking for the death penalty."[13] Undoubtedly, there must have been some confusion in the minds of all present if the district attorney's office proceeded as if this were a capital punishment case but did not seek the death penalty.

Voir dire is usually the first round of the fight. The prosecution and defense attempt to maneuver with various questions put to members of the jury pool. The goal is to find a jury that each lawyer feels will be most sympathetic to his client. Of course, this was 1949, and the art of jury selection was a long time in the future. Today, criminal law firms pay large amounts of fees to jury consultants to advise defense attorneys what to look for when considering a jury based on the crime. Also, these consultants may sit in court and study individual jury panel members to look for any type of reaction that they might have while other prospects are being questioned. This is especially true in what could be termed "high-profile" murder cases when the idea of "beyond a reasonable doubt" might be swayed by one juror based on his or her conception of the evidence or bias toward or against a defendant or a victim.

Needless to say, the *Commonwealth v. D'Amore* was a high-profile case in Delaware County, Pennsylvania, but the science of jury selection was not going to have any impact. It would be up to the individual lawyers, prosecution and defense to do the best each one could do to find a jury suited to their cases. That is probably why, in a January 4 article, the *Philadelphia Inquirer* termed the jury "a little out of place."[14] The reason the paper found the make-up of the jury so unusual? The jury panel consisted entirely of women, both the primary and alternate juries.

Prior to *voir dire*, defense attorney "Blumberg, made it quite evident that he wanted no men on the jury," and that is exactly what he got.[15] There were men in the jury pool, five of them to be exact, but due to defense challenges, they were all dismissed and sent home. It seemed that Blumberg had turned the thinking of the times—that woman were second-class citizens—on its head. And it also appears that Blumberg chose the right kind of women. All fourteen were married, and almost all had children and, in some cases, grandchildren of their own. From this point on, as far as the trial was concerned, girl power would be strictly enforced. To put it in a term very familiar today, it was a "dream team" of a jury.

There is nothing in the newspaper records to explain Prosecutor Lessy's reasoning for allowing the defense to pack the jury with all women. He had two ways to challenge prospective jurors. One was preemptory, which allowed him to object to a pool member for no stated reason, and the other was for cause, which allowed him to have a prospect dismissed for cause. One very important cause would be bias toward his case. It is not hard to see, even to a non-lawyer, that a woman might be biased for a defendant if that woman thought the defendant was acting to protect his mother from the abusive hands of her husband, even if it meant using deadly force.

Making an assumption based on no record about why Lessy allowed an all-female jury is nothing more than Monday-morning quarterbacking. It could be that Lessy thought the case was so strong—after all, he had the murder weapons and the confessions—that even a jury made up of only women would see that the boys were guilty. It could be that he never realized that some of the jury members were themselves in abusive relationships and that they could personally identify with the plight of Concetta D'Amore. Or it could be that his heart was just not in it when it came to prosecuting this particular case. Who knows? What is known is that, from a verdict standpoint, it may have been the biggest mistake he had ever made in his legal career.

Another issue that Lessy didn't seemed phased by was the fact that both he and the defense attorney, Blumberg, agreed to try both brothers together. Having both defendants tried together seems a strategic move from both sides. If one of the brothers is tried separately and found guilty, the defense has an excellent argument to say that the second brother (at his trial) had no part in the murder or, at best, that he was dragged into it by his guilty brother.

By trying the two brothers at the same trial, it would seem that the prosecution was really rolling the dice. It seemed to be a lose all or win all situation. Both brothers could have been convicted, or both could have been acquitted. It seems very unlikely that the jury would be able to reach a decision convicting one and acquitting the other. Again, there is no record of why the trial was not split. Maybe Lessy still believed his case was so strong that anything other than a guilty verdict was out of the question.

In the matter of trying both D'Amore brothers together, Matthew C. Stone, a practicing attorney who received his law degree from Pennsylvania State University, said that Lessy "probably would have agree to this, simply to avoid the potential for each brother to blame the other." As for the question of the all-female jury, Stone did think that this was a little strange. If he had been the prosecutor, he "would have tried to use preemptory challenges to empanel a jury with more gender diversity." Of course, the number and sex in the prospective jury pool would have a lot to do with it, according to Matt. It is all based on the characteristics of the majority called for jury duty on any given day. If, for example, a majority of the prospective jurors called that day were women, then "it would be difficult to avoid a situation where that characteristic describes most of the jury."[16]

Stone really did question the fact that the prosecutor asked for leniency because "the prosecutor usually wants the harshest punishment available…and asking for leniency…is usually on the agenda of a defense attorney who believes that he or she is losing the case."[17]

As for the trial judge allowing the defense to kiss each member of the jury, Matt thought "it very odd the the jurors allowed it [in that] it is hard to imagine that each and every member of the jury felt such a personal connection to the defense attorney."[18]

Trial Day One

The first day of the trial was taken up with administrative matters. *Voir dire* was concluded, and the jury was seated. Edith M. Force was appointed the forewoman since she was the first juror picked. (This is quite different from appointment of a jury foreperson today. After retiring to the jury room to start their deliberation, the members of the jury usually elect their foreperson.)

According to the description of the first day, as recorded in an article in the *Philadelphia Evening Bulletin*, "The slain man's widow, dressed all in black was seated beside her sons at the defense counsel's table. Overruling prosecution objections, Judge Toal granted her permission to sit there at

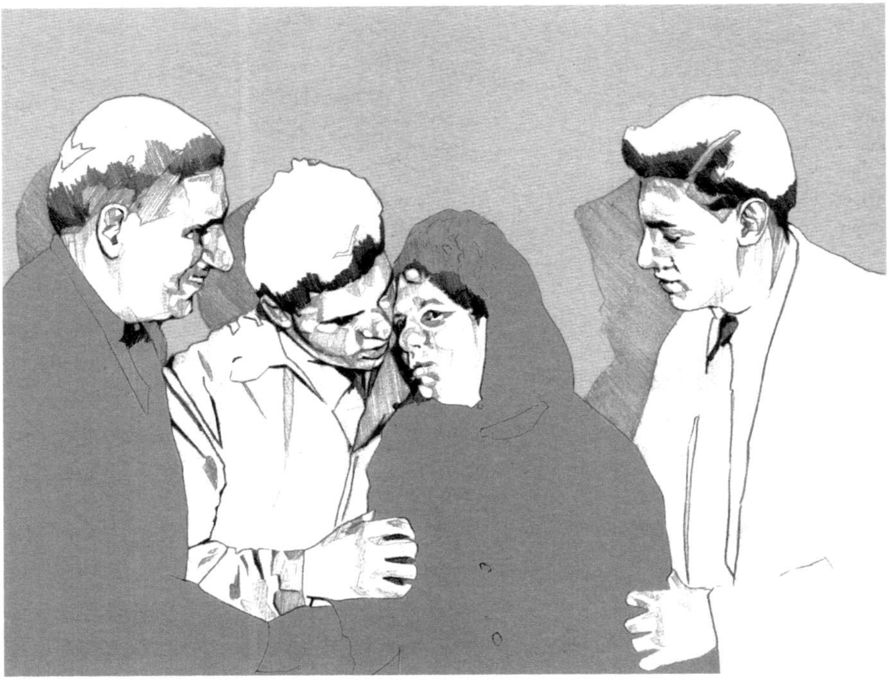

The D'Amore sons, Concetta and the defense attorney during the trial. *By Sally Klann.*

[defense attorney] Blumberg's request."[19] Again, there is no known reason why Judge Toal ruled in favor of the defense since the sight of the old, crippled mother, dressed in black mourning-style could surely be seen as a possible bias point that swayed the all-female jury. On the other hand, the chief of the Delaware County Detective Bureau, Fred Jack, sat next to Prosecutor Lessy at his table.

On the first day of the trial, both brothers entered a plea of not guilty to the two charges: murder in the first degree and conspiracy to commit murder. These pleas were direct contradictions to the story that both told the Marple Township police officers the night of the murder and to the testimony that Fred Jack had given at the Delaware County coroner's inquest on December 1, 1949, shortly after the crime had been committed.

Judge Toal recessed for the day at five o'clock in the afternoon. There was no real testimony of interest—that would come on the morning of the trial's second day.

Trial Day Two

Day two of the trial started out with the brothers' mother still seated next to them at the defense table and with legal maneuvering between the defense and the prosecution.

The first order of business was the statements of the two brothers. According to newspaper reports, Nicholas D'Amore's statement was entered into the record first. In the statement, he detailed what had taken place the evening of the murder, saying that when both boys arrived at the house, they were told about the beating by brother-in-law John Guianti. At this point, Nicholas instructed his brother John to go to Philadelphia and retrieve the second weapon. Upon his arrival back in Marple, John was told, "As soon as we see Pop, I'll shoot him with the rifle. If I miss, you use the shotgun." According to the remainder of the statement, the boys lay in wait for their father. When he returned, "Nicholas fired first…and then John let go with the shotgun."[20]

Probably the most shocking words that were read were those of Nicholas when he said, "He was six years old when he first got the idea that 'eventually' he would have to kill his father 'because of the way he treated all of us.'"[21] John's statement mirrored that of his brother.

At that point, Defense Attorney Blumberg moved to have both statements stricken from the record on the grounds that they were given under what he called "psychological duress." Judge Toal denied the motion.

Blumberg was much more successful when he moved to have the conspiracy to commit murder charge dropped. Judge Toal granted the motion on the grounds that "the only evidence of conspiracy was in the two brother's statements, which would not be accepted as such when the State could offer nothing in support."[22]

Then came the first big bombshell of the trial. Prosecutor Lessy called his first witness, John Guanti. Lessy was in trouble almost at once. Guanti was the ex-husband of Helen Bolenski, the sister of the defendants, and he was at the house the night of the murder. Lessy needed Guanti to identify the body of Benjamin D'Amore as the person whom the brothers had shot. Guanti testified that he could not identify the body as that of Benjamin D'Amore. According to Guanti, he and Helen Bolenski "were shown a body at the Media morgue after the slaying but could not identify it as D'Amore's."[23]

Next, Lessy called Helen Bolenski to the stand and asked her the same question. Could she identify the body of Benjamin D'Amore as the murder victim? Bolenski, parroting Guanti's testimony, said that she could not. It appears that Lessy had forgotten the first rule of questioning a witness. Never ask a question if you do not know the answer beforehand.

Lessy was able to mitigate some of Guanti's and Bolenski's testimonies by calling Marple Township chief of police Lester Downs to the stand. Downs was able to say that he had actually known D'amore for about fifteen years and had seen the body at both the scene of the crime and the morgue. Downs was "certain of his identification" that the dead man in question was, in fact, Benjamin D'Amore.[24]

Next in line for the prosecution was the Delaware County coroner's physician, Dr. Vincent A. Nacrelli. The prosecution, once again, found itself in a bit of a bind because Dr. Nacrelli was "unable to determine which gun caused D'Amore's death, as the entire left side of his face had been shot away."[25]

At this point, the proceedings were interrupted by the widow D'Amore, who was still dressed all in black and sitting beside her sons at the defense table. The sight of her dead husband's bloody clothes and the two murder weapons were too much for her. Crying and screaming, she was escorted out of the courtroom until she calmed down. Apparently, a more tranquil Mrs. D'Amore was allowed back and retook her seat next to her sons at the defense table.

The only other witness on day two was the county's chief detective, Fred Jack. Chief Jack testified to having seen "a two-inch circular bruise on her [Concetta D'Amore's] cheek when he arrived at the house."[26] He went on to the recap the testimony that he had given at the December 1, 1949 coroner's inquest.

The day ended with some more legal machinations on the part of the prosecution. Lessy entered an objection based on some remarks made by the defense related to the continued abuse that the family had suffered at the hands of their now dead father. After hearing arguments, Judge Toal ruled that "the evidence dealing with the father's treatment of the mother was admissible, but could be used by the jury only in fixing the degree of guilt should a guilty verdict be returned [and that] this evidence must not be used to determine the guilt or innocence of the defendants."[27]

With that, the prosecution rested, and the trial day ended. The next day would bring the first mention that the alleged abuse suffered all those years might not have been the real motive for the murder.

Trial Day Three

The D'Amore trial was knocked off the top of the fold headline story by an accident that had taken place on the Delaware River in Chester, Pennsylvania. The Chester-Bridgeport ferryboat *Lackawanna* had been rammed by a freighter mid-stream, resulting in one death and three injuries. In 1950, the Chester-Bridgeport boats were the only means of getting from Pennsylvania to New Jersey once out of the Philadelphia city limits.

When Judge Toal called the courtroom to order, it was the time for the defense to present its case in chief. The day would be all about abuse.

In what newspapers referred to as a state of shock and horror, accompanied by head shaking and audible gasps from both the jury box and the packed court room, the D'Amore children testified to the unspeakable abuse they had endured at the hands of their father.

Nicholas was the first to take the stand. He said:

> *My first day at school, I got afraid for some reason and ran home. When my father asked Mom why I was not in school and she told him, he grabbed her and started beating her... When I got a poor report card, he would beat me and mom both and tell her it was her fault...He would often chain me to a post in the cellar over night without any food. When he caught Mom bringing food down to me, he would beat her too.*[28]

According to Nicholas, he and his brother John were made to get up very early in the morning, before school, and work in their father's nursery. After school, they were expected to do the same thing late into the evening.

John was called to testify next. He said:

> *I would be so sleepy in school, I would doze over my lessons and the teacher would send a note home and he would beat me and my mom... When I was 14, he put me in the cellar for nearly two weeks to punish me for something and he told me, "You deserve to sleep with the rats."*[29]

Helen Bolenski, the boys' sister, took the stand. She testified:

> *Once he chained me in the cellar overnight. He tied my hands to a stovepipe so I couldn't sit down. Mother tried to sneak food to me. He caught her and threw her down the cellar steps...I remember my brothers and I coming home from school and my father putting tacks on the floor. He made us*

> *kneel on them as punishment for something we had done. He even beat us on holiday.*[30]

An employee of D'Amore at the nursery, Justino Palestini, told the court that he had once seen his boss club his wife with the handle of a hoe. To this, Judge Toal inquired about why the witness and others looking on did not interfere. When Palestini said that they did not want to, Toal labeled them all "a fine bunch of men [that] should have hit him on the head with the hoe yourself."

Sometime during the testimony about the numerous incidents of abuse, Judge Toal took over from defense attorney Blumberg and, as reported in the *Philadelphia Evening Bulletin*, started asking his own questions of the witnesses, particularly Helen Bolenski. He said, "Now, I want to ask some questions about these beatings: what did he beat you with and where did he hit you?"

Helen replied, "My father often used a belt buckle in the beatings, sometimes his fists. He wore a heavy signet ring on one finger and often he kicked me."

"Where were you struck?"

"On the body, face, head—anywhere we couldn't duck."

When Helen told him that no member of the family ever sought medical treatment or called the police, Judge Toal said, "I cannot understand it that there never was a broken bone or a cut requiring a doctor's attention or a complaint to the police if this beating was as continuous as you say."

"He told us that if we ever told anybody about him beating us or complained to police, we would never live another day."

Defense Attorney Blumberg apparently wanted his witness back, so he filed an objection with Judge Toal. Judge Toal denied the objection and, according to the *Evening Bulletin*, continued to ask Helen additional questions.

The brothers' and sister's testimony about the abuse was corroborated by several non-family members who testified that they had seen bruises and marks on the children over periods of times.

Also testifying that day were a local justice of the peace and a local attorney who said that, at a time about three years in the past, two of the D'Amore boys and one of his sisters (the justice did not recall which children had come before him) came to him and wanted to swear out a warrant against their father, the boys for abuse and the girl because her father would not give her any of her clothes in order for her to leave home. The justice told the court that he talked the children out of taking legal action on the grounds that he would speak directly to the father. The local attorney recalled that Concetta

D'Amore, along with one of her daughters, came to him for advice on how to handle Benjamin, but after consultation on the matter, neither woman took any legal suggestions.

Once again, it is impossible to know how different the fate of the D'Amore family might have been if the justice of the peace had allowed for the warrant or if the two D'Amore women had taken the attorney's advice. At best, the two sons might never have felt forced to end their father's life, and at worse, the police would have had cause to keep an eye on what was happening within the D'Amore household.

At some time during the day's court session, Concetta D'Amore was called to the stand by the defense attorney. It fell on Mrs. D'Amore to speak about her life with Benjamin.

According to the *Chester Times*, Concetta described the scene:

> *My husband called from his upstairs bedroom.* "Gualio [boy], *where are my socks?" I told him they were in a bureau drawer, but the socks in the drawer weren't the ones he wanted. I went upstairs to get the socks he wanted and wash them. But he started to hit me. He punched me in the head, in the face, in the back—anyplace. He pulled my hair and kicked me and hurt my leg. He took off his strap* [belt] *and whipped me. The beating lasted about half an hour.*

"When did it start?" the district attorney asked.

"When I started having children."

"How many times did he lick you in one week?"

"Why, every day."

"Do you remember what happened when you were carrying Yolanda?"

"My husband gave me medicine to lose the baby."

On cross-examination, Prosecutor R. Paul Lessy surprised the courtroom when he started to question Mrs. D'Amore about her husband's will. According to the *Chester Times*, Lessy asked about a will that made Mrs. D'Amore the sole benefactor should Benjamin die. Lessy went on to point out that at Mr. D'Amore's death, the estate was to be divided in three equal portions that would go to the remaining D'Amore son and his two sisters. Nicholas and John, the two sons who were on trial for the murder of their father, had been cut out of the will. Each would receive five dollars. Mrs. D'Amore said that while that was how the will was written at Benjamin's death, neither Nicholas nor John knew about their respective positions in the document. Apparently, Lessy may have been trying to plant seeds in the collective minds of the jury that either the sons knew about the will and were angry with their father for his slight or they did not know about the will and murdered him for, what they thought, was their part of the estate. Lessy, it seems, did not want to pursue the issue of abuse since it would make the little old woman on the stand a more sympathetic figure than she already was.

Day Four

The business of the court on the fourth day was hearing expert testimony, hearing closing arguments and giving the all-female jury the charges.

Both the prosecution and the defense presented "expert" witnesses. The problem with expert witnesses is that they very rarely, if ever, agree. They are not supposed to. Truth be told, expert witnesses are really just "hired guns" paid to substantiate the case of either the prosecution or the defense. There is nothing wrong with that—it is the way the adversarial system of justice works. The primary weakness of expert witnesses seems to be that they confuse the jury because the average jury has no real idea what the expert is talking about. It isn't because the average jury is made up of stupid people; it is because the average jury never really comes in contact, on a day-to-day basis, with the topics about which the expert is talking. In some cases, it is questionable whether juries even consider expert testimony when they are deliberating. As experts drone on and on about their area of expertise, it is fair to assume that a majority of the jurors are looking out the courtroom's windows thinking, "What am I doing here on such a beautiful day?"

In the case of the D'Amore brothers, the question for the experts was were the boys insane at the time they executed their father?

It goes without saying that the two "experts" for the defense, Dr. O.M. Ornsteen and Dr. Gabrial Schwrz, both psychiatrists from Philadelphia, said yes they were. Actually, they did not think the two brothers were always insane, just temporarily insane, and just between 6:00 p.m. and 11:30 p.m., which was exactly the time they were at the D'Amore home awaiting the return of their father.

In present-day Pennsylvania, two state statutes guide the insanity plea. The first, 18 Pa. Cons. Stat §315(a) and (b), define insanity, and the second, 236 Pa. Code Rule 568, outlines the legal procedure that must be followed for the defense to enter a plea of insanity. First, a pre-trial omnibus motion must be entered stating the extent of the insanity, the time period of the insanity and the names of witnesses that would be called to testify concerning the insanity. There are no available records to verify that any of this was done at the D'Amore trial.

Drs. Ornsteen and Schwarz testified that the brothers suffered "catathymic crises," which they described as a "subconscious state that made the defendants unable to tell right from wrong."[31] The lack of trial transcripts make it unknown if either Dr. Ornsteen or Dr. Schwarz explained, in detail, what a catathymic crisis actually was or how the brothers were affected by it. The best way to describe a catathymic crisis is to relate it to an earthquake. The San Andreas Fault runs almost the entire north–south length of the state of California. Over the years, numerous major quakes have occurred because of it. The fault is the border between two tectonic plates, the Pacific Plate and the North American Plate. Over hundreds of years, these plates sliding against each other create extreme pressure until, at one point, the pressure gets so extreme that the fault brakes, and the result is an earthquake.

Now how does this apply to the D'Amore murder? Well, the sliding of the plates together is the same as the acts of abuse that were testified to by the brothers, their sister and also their mother. In between the abusive acts, the fear of and hate for the father built up just like the fault line's pressure. The breaking point was on the evening of the murder, when the boys found that their father had beaten their mother over a pair of dirty socks. The resultant event, just like an earthquake, was the killing of Benjamin D'Amore. According to a 2005 study of catathymic crises by John Jay College of Criminal Justice professor Louis B. Schleslinger, from a 1992 paper by J.R. Maloy entitled "Violent Attachments," "The tension build-up, usually lasting months to a year, is finally cathected, and the intolerable feeling of being controlled by the malevolent object [the victim] is reversed. Absolute control of the object, as the source of persecutory distress is acted out through violence."[32]

Next, as rebuttal witnesses, came the prosecution "experts," Drs. Charles Rupp and Joseph C. Yaskin, both from the University of Pennsylvania. (There is no mention of what either of the good doctors did at the university or of what educational discipline they practiced.)

As was expected, both witnesses testified that both brothers knew what was right and what was wrong at the time they pulled the triggers on their respective murder weapons. Both doctors went on to say, "The general theory of catathymic crises has never received adequate substantiation."[33]

It was now time for closing arguments. The prosecutor, R. Paul Lessy spoke first. He said, "The Bible says that 'He who smiteth his father or mother shall be put to death.' But anyone not affected by the testimony of cruelty—and at times excessive cruelty—is not being intellectually honest. This case does not demand the extreme penalty of death."[34]

This statement must have been somewhat confusing to the jury. Here was an assistant district attorney, tasked with putting on the best possible case aimed at bringing about the strictest punishment allowable by law, asking for mercy for the defendants because of the actions of the victim. Explaining his unusual start, Lessy would later say, "I decided not to ask for the supreme penalty at 3:30 a.m. yesterday, after I had reviewed all the testimony…it is my belief that the lily had been gilded and the pot blackened."[35]

After his plea for mercy, Lessy, for the next two hours, told the jury that what the boys did was murder, that they never should have taken the law into their own hands and that, instead of blowing their dad's head off, it probably would have been best just to call the cops.

The defense attorney, Albert Blumberg, went next. There is no information on just how long Blumberg spoke, but it is noted that he reminded the jury of the family's previous testimony concerning abuse at the hands of the father. Like Lessy, Blumberg invoked God as a player in this case. Blumberg told the jury that God may have intervened to help Concetta D'Amore in her hour of need. "Ask yourself," Blumberg told the jury, "if at this point, God did not hear her and take a hand."[36] (This may have been one of the first times in Delaware County judicial history that God was noted as being involved in a conspiracy to commit murder.)

Reminding the jury that Prosecutor Lessy had taken death off the table, Blumberg said, "Death has gone out the window and I'm hopeful that by the time this is finished the entire case will be out of the window."[37]

Trying to attack any idea that the stories of abuse by the D'Amore family had been exaggerated to mitigate the crime, Blumberg told the jury, "Suppose it has been exaggerated…take off 90 percent of it and that alone will convince you ladies of the jury what a hell there must have been in that Marple Township household all those years."[38]

In what was Blumberg's end to his closing, he implored the jury to "send these boys back to take care of their crippled mother. Let them help her forget the terror of the past 25 years. These boys have been punished enough already."[39]

Pointing to Concetta D'Amore, he continued:

> *Were the lines in that woman's face caused by her 52 years or by her unbearable suffering? How many years of tears were needed to give her eyes that sorrowful look? Yet she still proudly has the love that her sons gave her.*

> *The one unusual thing about this murder case is that nobody shed any tears over the deceased. His epitaph should be: "He won't beat Mom anymore."*[40]

And with that, the trial part came to an end. It was now the jury's turn to take over. But before that, Judge Toal charged the jury members for one hour and forty-five minutes. Their decision was to hang on the testimony by the experts. He told the jury that the fact that the boys had murdered their father was not the central issue when it came to a verdict. The central issue was whether they knew right from wrong when they each pulled the triggers. The central issue was the possible temporary insanity at the time they gunned down Benjamin D'Amore. Based on that central issue, the jury could reach one of three verdicts: first-degree murder, second-degree manslaughter or acquittal. He then told them to "get a good night's rest and begin thinking about the verdict tomorrow."[41] He sent them home.

Day Five

At 10:00 a.m., the jury started its deliberation. By 12:18 p.m., the jury was back in the courtroom with a decision. Jude Toal asked, "Has the jury reached a verdict?"

Forewoman Edith Force replied, "Yes, we have reached a verdict."

"What is your verdict?"

"Not guilty."[42]

The three hundred or so spectators in the courtroom broke into applause.

Prosecutor Lessy walked over to the defense table and shook hands with Blumberg and the two D'Amore brothers. He placed his hand on each brother's shoulder and said, "Please boys, try to be good from here on in."[43]

As the two brothers remained at the defense table, Judge Toal spoke to the jury:

> *I told you jurors that this was an unlawful killing. I still say so. Under the law only a lunatic can be excused for murder. But over the past 30 years a new idea has developed which was expounded to you during this trial* [the theory of a catathymic crises]. *This theory was developed by the two psychiatrists for the defense and it is good that we have new ideas.*[44]

After that, Defense Attorney Blumberg asked the judge for permission to kiss the jury. Judge Toal said that it was "OK with the court."[45] Blumberg approached the jury and kissed each and every member. He then took the D'Amore brothers to the bench and had them shake hands with the judge. Judge Toal admonished the two. "Boys," he said, "you have had a fair trial. The jury has acquitted you. Go out now and be good boys."[46]

Afterward, the D'Amore brothers left the courtroom, gathered their belongings in a nearby office, walked out of the building and, with their mother and some other relatives, got into a waiting automobile driven by John Guanti. All along the way, from the courtroom to the car, congratulations were offered by courthouse employees, friends and strangers. The trial of the century, at least for Delaware County, Pennsylvania, had ended. And, it seemed, everybody was happy with the verdict.

8
BACK STORY

There is always a back story. Back stories are the way people express their opinions about what they think happened and why they think it happened.This is especially true when it comes to major crime events. The O.J. Simpson case had a back story, actually several. The Casey Anthony case had a back story, and the Jon Benet Ramsey case had a back story.

The D'Amore murder case was no different. There was a back story swirling around the evidence and facts that were presented in court. In the D'Amore case, the back story had to do with motive. It was made very clear to everybody who went to or read about the trial that the main motive for the murder was how the brothers wanted to end the years of abuse at the hands of their father. Their motive was fear. The jury bought that motive when it acquitted Nicholas and John. Some individuals more closely related to the inside workings of the D'Amore family feel that the real motive was not fear but greed and that the abuse, while true, may have been exaggerated and used as an excuse to commit the murder.

There is a thought among some present-day family members that Benjamin was well off. (It is difficult to determine what "well off" was in 1949. According to a February 18, 1951 report published by the Census Bureau for the United States Department of Commerce, the average family income was $3,100. Families that were headed by self-employed individuals, as were the D'Amores, made $2,300 per year.) Though research turned up no record of it, Benjamin was supposed to have several real estate holdings other than the nursery throughout Delaware County. Some individuals

Conspiracy? *By Sally Klann.*

typed both Nicholas and John as rich kids riding around in nice cars, but once again, there is no way to substantiate that.

The primary back story for this case revolves around the idea that members of the family—including Concetta, Nicholas, John and Helen—were interested in getting their hands on the estate. John Guanti's name also comes into the picture at this point. John Guanti, it is said, was either a partner in the nursery business with Benjamin or he was an employee of Benjamin's. John's alleged desire to take part ownership in the business is a central argument in the greed-motivated back story. One point that is somewhat confusing is that, at the time of the murder, Helen and John had divorced and Helen was, in fact, married to a gentleman named Bolenski. (There is no record of John Bolenski's involvement in any of the events leading up to the murder or during the subsequent trial.) After the acquittal, Helen divorced Bolenski and remarried John Guanti. One thing is true: Guanti was at the D'Amore homestead the night of the murder. Taken together, this is a great group of facts for any conspiracy theorist to work with.

Why was John Guanti at the house on the night of the murder? After Nicholas sent his brother John to the Parkside neighborhood of Philadelphia to get another gun, what happened in the D'Amore house? When John D'Amore returned with the second weapon, there may and have been several hours' wait until Benjamin arrived home. Were the boys, their sister Helen, John Guanti and Concetta hatching the plot to kill the father that night? Written on a piece of paper used for research were the words, John Guanti said, "the third shot got Pop." Was there a third shot? If so, that means that the first two shots either missed Benjamin, or if they struck their target, they were not fatal. Did one of the boys shoot twice? Was there a third shooter inside the house at an upstairs window with a downward trajectory who actually fired the kill shot? If there was a separate, third shot, who was the third shooter?

It seems that the law enforcement agencies that investigated the shooting went no further than to take the boys' word that they had killed their father that night. The boys were charged with conspiracy to commit murder, but that charge was dismissed during the trial. No other persons—not Concetta, John Guanti or Helen—were ever charged with any crimes related to the primary one. If there was a conspiracy to murder Benjamin for his estate, it was left unpunished and evaporated into time.

Another back story to quite a few murders is revenge. Obviously, the D'Amore murder had a certain revenge aspect to it if people buy into the abuse motive. The boys murdered their father in order to avenge his cruelty to the rest of the family.

There was an interesting and apparently clandestine document that surfaced during Concetta's testimony under cross-examination by Prosecutor R. Paul Lessy. It was the questions about the "mystery will," the will that left everything to Concetta upon the death of Benjamin and, upon the death of Concetta, left everything split equally among the two sisters, Helen and Yolanda, and one son, Anthony. Nicholas and John each were left five dollars apiece. Recall that Concetta testified that neither Nicholas nor John knew anything about the will. (There was no mention of whether Helen, Yolanda or Anthony knew about it.)

However, speculating that the brothers did know that they were virtually cut out of the D'Amore estate, did the brothers murder their father, not out of fear or greed, but out of revenge for his obvious financial slight?

One other point can be made about the mystery will: why did Benjamin exclude Nicholas and John from their fair share of the D'Amore estate? Could it have been that he was somehow aware that they intended to do him harm? By leaving them a combined total of ten dollars, did he wield the ultimate and final control and punishment over his two murderous sons?

But was there such a will anyway?

According to a Saturday, May 20, 1950 article in the *Chester Times*, "D'Amore left no will and the estate has been administered by the First National Bank of Media."[47] At the request of the bank, the decision on who would share in the estate was handled by the Delaware County Orphans Court since Benjamin had died intestate. Apparently, the estate amounted to $80,000, of which $50,000 was in real estate.

Orphans Court judge E. Leroy van Roden presided. He ruled, "Because the sons were found to have been temporarily insane, the killing was neither willful nor unlawful."[48]

The newspaper noted that the estate was broken down, so "D'Amore's widow will receive one-third of the estate. Each of the 5 children will receive two-fifteenths of the estate."[49] Both Nicholas and John walked away with $10,000.00. (In today's money, based on a 3.5 percent rate of inflation, that would be $99,496.61.)

As for the mystery will, it remains for the curious to question how R. Paul Lessy came up with the information about it. Why did Concetta testify that the will did exist but that neither Nicholas nor John knew anything about it?

In the end, if the back stories are true, and greed or revenge was the primary motive for the murder, it appears that all members of the D'Amore family got what they wanted. Of course, it can be said that Benjamin D'Amore never got what he wanted. All he got was a kill shot to the head.

9
THE SKELETON IN THE CLOSET (REDUX)

One of the most interesting things about this case is Benjamin D'Amore's first name. He was christened "Panfilo" in his home country of Italy. In Italian, it means "a friend to all." The fourteenth-century Italian poet Giovanni Boccaccio, in his work *Decameron*, named one of the characters Panfilo. This Panfilo was in love with love.

Even Benjamin's last name, D'Amore, translates into the English word "love." Put both names together, and Panfilo D'Amore can be loosely translated into "a loving friend to all." Sometimes, however, you just can't judge a book by its cover.

Surely, when she was born, and as she grew to adulthood, Concetta wanted only a happy marriage, a good husband and a fine family. Obviously, neither Benjamin nor Concetta realized when they married in their native land of Italy that the marriage would end in tragic death.

When they decided to leave Italy and move to the United States, they did not know that instead of hope and success, their lives in the United States would bring only pain, sorrow and death. They did not know as they boarded the steamship, their last port of call, that a nursery in Marple Township, Pennsylvania, would be where Benjamin would spend his last moments on earth. They did not know that the trip would bring sadness and misunderstanding to the entire family.

By all accounts, Panfilo D'Amore was a monster, not a loving friend of all. In a personal conversation with longtime Marple Township resident and school classmate of Yolanda D'Amore Jack Smith, he said that many times

The D'Amores' American nightmare. *By Sally Klann.*

"Yolanda was plain scared just to go home after school, just very scared of her father"[50]

Ted Muehlmatt, another resident of Marple, agreed with Jack Smith. He was a schoolmate of both Nicholas and John D'Amore, and he said that both boys told him that their father "would make them work in the fields until very late at night." Muehlmatt went on to say that both boys were left back a grade several times due to poor schoolwork and, he thought, because neither boy actually graduated from school. (This corroborates the court testimony of both Nicholas and John when they said that they often fell asleep in school because they were made to work both early in the morning and late into the night. The fact that their schoolwork suffered was another cause for Benjamin's abusive handling of them.)

Both Smith and Muehlmatt mentioned that they couldn't recall one person feeling sorry for Benjamin D'Amore's death. They said that the public consensus was that the murder was a "mercy killing" performed to protect the family.

Terming the crime a "mercy killing" might be a stretch. After all, a mercy killing does evoke the idea that those committing the act have compassion for the person whose life is being terminated. Nowhere in the D'Amore murder can compassion be considered an emotional motivation for the shooting. The argument that the brothers had compassion for their mother after that day's beating does not hold up. Benjamin D'Amore wasn't killed out of compassion; he was executed out of fear and rage. It seems that the public's consideration of the event as a mercy killing may be a way of rationalizing and condoning murder because, in the end, the public perceived that the D'Amore family was relieved of its collective suffering.

Not everybody in Delaware County felt the boys were justified in what they did. In the Friday, January 13, 1950 edition of the *Chester Times*, county resident John J. Meehan wrote a letter to the editor expressing his ideas about the murder, the all-female jury, the verdict and the judge's admonishment to the boys to "go home and be good boys." Meehan did not hide his thoughts when he wrote:

> *Despite the addled-headed verdict of the emotional "mama jury," the D'Amore "boys" are murderers in my book. If they did not like their father and his manners, why did they not leave him? The "all mama" jury can sit on the question, if they are not allergic to logic. So, pass the lipstick daughter, "mama jury" has fallen for the defense attorney, father D'Amore got what he deserved and the "boys" will please return to Sunday school, conscience and all.*[51]

Panfilo D'Amore's family burial plot. *By Sally Klann.*

Meehan's letter points out a lot of what can be termed the opinions of the time, and while he may not have known it, he hit on several issues that caused the murder. Meehan diminishes the severity of the abuse as simply an example of Benjamin's "manners." He seems to see the abuse as something that the boys could have left behind them if they had just escaped the homestead. He belittles the intelligence of women and the bond that mothers instinctively have with their children. It may be a fair conclusion that such thinking was, in the big picture, a contributing factor to what happened at the D'Amore homestead that night.

Of course, as time passed, the thoughts of the people of Delaware County moved on to other matters. New crimes were committed, new criminals were caught by the police, police laid charges, charges were turned into indictments, indictments turned into trials and trials tuned into either convictions or acquittals. Life went on.

The nursery became a patch of overgrown trees and bushes strewn with junk. The site where the murder house once rested is now a multiplex movie theater. The rest of the area is taken up by a strip mall.

On Wednesday, January 11, 1950, the *Chester Times* printed a follow-up story about the D'Amore family. It had been a little over fifty days since the murder of their father. The boys were now looking for a normal life. Normal life was what they had prayed for all during the trial, and it was what they got after the acquittal. It is, however, highly speculative what a normal life could be for two

The site of the murder house as it looks today. *By Sally Klann.*

sons who had, in the span of fifty days, murdered their father, been arrested, spent time in jail, faced first-degree murder charges, been found to have been temporarily insane and, in the end, been allowed to walk.

It appears that one of the brothers, Nicholas, made good use of prayer, as he spent the night before the jury was to reach a verdict asking for God's help. As to the acquittal, Nicholas said that "it was what I had prayed for." Referred to in the article as the "quiet 26-year old brother," Nicholas went on to recall that he "was afraid to look at the jury as it brought in the verdict" and that he "sucked in air that [his] heart felt like it was going to burst."[52]

Good boys were what both the judge and the prosecutor told them to be, "and that's what they hope to be…forever. After years of beating, running away, tearful returns, trying to protect 'mom', the boys hope they are home to stay—all under one serene roof."[53]

It was hard on their mother, too. Difficulty eating, difficulty sleeping, walking the floor, bad memories and solicitous friends had kept Concetta awake all night.

On the other hand, John, whom the article termed "less of a worrier than [his brother] Nick," was up bright and early and spent his morning repairing his car. Now unemployed because he had left a job with the American Forestry Service, John planned "to stay home with 'Mom' and help his brother-in-law, John Guanti, run his dead father's business"[54]

When asked about his future plans, Nick, a self-admitted "jack of all trades and master of none," said that he "had to keep busy." He liked carpentry but not wallpapering. He hoped for two things: that "he might get his old job back as a sheet metal worker at Budd's" and that "by the end of the week, his three-year-old daughter would be back home." Relatives had told the child that her dad was at work.[55]

In a rather touching and sentimental end to the article, the boys admitted to being homesick "in solitary cells as they listened to Christmas carols which blared over the loud speakers in the jail."[56]

While the newspaper did admit that the murder was a "unique case of dual patricide," the article went on to say that "the brothers today are only grateful boys who admitted they're happy and lucky that the all-mother jury 'saw it our way.'"[57]

Even now, in 2015, the D'Amore murder remains such a strange case. Many things stand out. The way the community perceived John and Nicholas D'Amore is one of the most interesting. Everybody called them "boys." The judge called them boys, the prosecutor called them boys, the defense lawyer called them boys, the expert witnesses called them boys, the cops called them boys and even John Guanti called them boys. In fact, neither one was a boy. At the time of the murder, Nicholas was twenty-six years old and John was twenty-two years old. They were the D'Amore men. Yet for some reason, they were still boys in the minds of all those involved in any way with the case.

Could it be that the supporters of John and Nicholas, knowing full well that they were admitted killers, found it easier to rationalize their support by seeing them as boys rather than grown adults? Could it be that grown adults don't go around killing their fathers, but boys may not have the good sense to figure out a logical way to resolve a situation? After all, boys do resolve wrongs by fighting while grown men usually resolve wrongs by thinking. Could it be that the brothers were considered "slow" and acted like boys instead of grown men? Could it be that, in the eyes of the public, men did not allow themselves to be abused by other men while boys had no defense, especially if the other man was their father? The nickname does seem to play into the fact that John and Nicholas D'Amore may have been acquitted because the all-female jury saw them as boys, unable to defend themselves or their mother.

Of interest is the way the public was said to have openly supported the D'Amore family. Most of the time, the general public does not support a murderous act. Even today, when instant news brings the most intimate of details regarding a brutal crime, the general public will often side with the victim. In even the most ordinary of physical crimes, the public always seems to cry out for justice for the victim. As much as Americans like to criticize their legal system, they do believe that, in the end, the victim or the victim's family will find some satisfaction when the person brought to trial is convicted.

This was, most assuredly, not the case when it came to the D'Amore murder. According to records, when the verdict of acquittal was announced, the crowd in the courtroom went wild with applause and delight. In the hallways of the courthouse and in the streets outside the building, the announcement was met with delight. People rushed to the newly freed brothers to give their congratulations on a job well done. The newspapers gave the impression that John and Nicholas were just two lucky guys who were so happy to be home after having spent fifty days away from their home for no reason other than that they had just murdered their father. If all this is to be believed, John and Nicholas D'Amore were the two most beloved temporarily insane father murders in the history of Delaware County. What makes this love-fest even stranger is that it all came at a time when beating one's wife was not really a big deal.

Another issue open to speculation is the trial itself. The all-female jury; the grieving wife and mother; the prosecutor who didn't want the death penalty and congratulated the brothers after their acquittal; the experts who testified that the boys were temporarily insane at the time of the murder; the defense attorney who worked *voir dire* to the point that only women were seated on the jury; and the judge who told the boys to be good lads from that point on and then allowed the defense attorney to kiss and hug the jury—taken all together, it appears that nobody was really interested in trying the boys and that everybody was just plain happy the boys got away with it.

When all the facts about the D'Amore murder, the abuse, the trial and the public reaction are taken as a whole, can conclusions be drawn about people's idea of crime in general? Is the way the public reacts to crime, especially murder, an offshoot of social dynamics?

Discounting the fact that nowhere in our legal system is "justice for the victim" ever called for and that once the victim draws his or her final breath, he or she is nothing more than evidence that a crime has taken place, public opinion almost always falls on the side of the wronged person. The individual or individuals who committed the criminal act are never championed by anyone except members of the defense bar.

It is a question of social interplay. People always want to be on the side of the poor, innocent victim. It is human nature at its most basic. It is the continuing story of good versus evil, and nobody wants to be on the side of evil. That is why juries that acquit defendants in high-profile murder cases are usually thought of as having made the wrong decision and, in some cases, are publically vilified for letting criminals back on the street.

The D'Amore murder case was unique among murder cases in that the public perception was completely reversed. The majority of people thought that the two sons were the victims, along with their sisters and mother. The public believed that their father, Benjamin D'Amore, was the devil himself. It was as if the two boys were avenging angels sent by God to right the wrong that their father had, for years, foisted upon the rest of the D'Amore family. To the public—and some would say, to the lawyers, the jury and the judge—they were just two white knights arriving in the nick of time to do battle with the evil foe for the sake of the D'Amore kingdom. They were a couple of "good boys" being treated as if they had toppled over the neighbor's outhouse on mischief night instead of committing the capital crime of patricide.

Of course, all this begs the question: was the victim, Benjamin D'Amore, ever considered in all this? By seeing the murderers as the innocent victims, did the public as a whole take both before-the-fact and after-the-fact roles in the crime? Looking at all the facts, a yes conclusion is not beyond the realm of possibility.

Testimony given at trial by workers on D'Amore's nursery corroborated the families' stories of beatings at the hands of the father. Individuals alive today who knew the D'Amore children substantiate the tales that they were made to work early in the morning before school and late into the night after school. Yet in a time of live and let live, nobody made any attempt to notify the authorities about what was going on inside the D'Amore homestead. Obviously, it is not certain that intervention would have eliminated the murder altogether, but the lack of community interest just seemed to create a larger-than-life identity around the case of Benjamin D'Amore to the point that nobody really cared that he was murdered. The general perception of D'Amore as a monster became reality.

Today, the D'Amore case would probably turn out much differently. Experts in psychiatry and social factors would surely testify that the D'Amore boys knew exactly what they were doing when they pulled the trigger, ruling out catathymic crises or any other mental disorder. Experts in family abuse situations would surely testify that, while the D'Amore family may have suffered tragically at the hands of their father, the boys were still not in any position to take his life. Experts on jury selection would have studied the jury pool and made recommendations on whom and whom not to choose. The prosecutor would have surely objected to an all-female jury on the grounds of inherent bias, and D'Amore's widow would never have been allowed to occupy a seat at the defense table beside her suspect sons. Today, it would be a good bet that both D'Amore boys would have been convicted of first-degree murder and would have spent the rest of their lives in prison.

But what is not a sure bet is that the general public would not react in the same way it did in 1949 and 1950. It is quite possible, all things considered, that people would still perceive Benjamin D'Amore as a monster and believe that his murder was exactly what he deserved.

If a person were to try to reach a conclusion about the D'Amore family tragedy by searching through the facts, testimony and evidence concerning the real reason Benjamin was murdered, they would find it hard to land on a real result. Some may believe the true motive was abuse, while some may

The Delaware County Courthouse. *By Sally Klann.*

The D'Amore family. *By Sally Klann.*

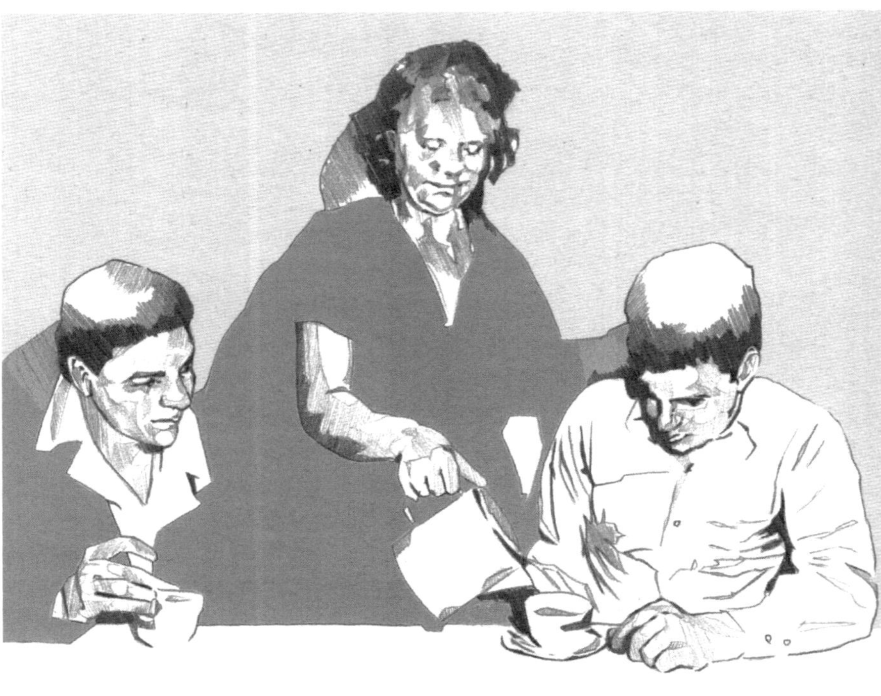

Concetta and two of her sons at home after the trial. *By Sally Klann.*

come out on the side of greed. Some may even believe that it was a little bit of both. There is no real answer, and there will probably never be an answer. That is why it remains an interesting mystery.

In the end, it all happened in 1949, not in the present. The morning sun shone golden on the front steps of the Delaware County Courthouse, Panfilo Benjamin D'Amore was dead, the boys and the rest of the family were safe from his abusing hands, John and Nick were both $10,000 richer, John Guanti got to run the nursery and, in the eyes of the general public, justice was served. The story of the D'Amore family could not have ended any better than it did.

Appendix

THOSE INVOLVED

The D'Amore Family

Anthony D'Amore	Benjamin and Concetta's son
Benjamin D'Amore	the father and murder victim
Concetta D'Amore	Benjamin's wife
Dawn D'Amore Yankanich	Benjamin and Concetta's granddaughter
Helen D'Amore	Benjamin and Concetta's daughter
John D'Amore	Benjamin and Concetta's son and shooter
Nicholas D'Amore	Benjamin and Concetta's son and shooter
Yolanda D'Amore Maggio	Benjamin and Concetta's daughter
John Guanti	Helen's husband and Benjamin's son in law

Law Enforcement

Joseph Baker	Springfield Township police officer
Lester Downs	Marple Township police chief
Fred Jack	Delaware County Detectives chief
Newton Kerber	Marple Township police officer
Clarence Orr	Marple Township police officer

APPENDIX

The Court

Albert Blumberg	D'Amore defense attorney
Ernest Dupille	Marple Township district justice
Harold I. Ervin	Court of Common Pleas judge
Edith M. Force	jury foreperson
R. Paul Lessy	assistant DA and prosecutor
William R. Toal	trial judge
E. Leroy van Roden	Delaware County Orphans' Court judge

Witnesses and Others

Harry Meyers	criminologist and D'Amore neighbor
Ernest Muehlmatt	witness and neighbor
Vincent A. Nacrelli	Delaware County coroner
M. A. Oresteen	witness for the defense, psychiatry
Charles Rupp	expert witness, psychiatry
Gabriel Schwartz	witness for the defense, psychiatry
Joseph C. Yaskins	expert witness, psychiatry

NOTES

Introduction

1. *Parson v. State.*
2. *Daubert v. Merrell Dow Pharmaceutical, Inc.*

Chapter 2

3. Spinogatti, e-mail to the author.

Chapter 4

4. May, *Meaning of Anxiety*.
5. Maier, e-mail to the author.
6. May, *Meaning of Anxiety*.
7. Ibid.
8. Pickrin, *Psychology Book*.

Chapter 6

9. Fahy, e-mail to the author.
10. Ibid.
11. Ibid.

Chapter 7

12. *Philadelphia Evening Bulletin*, "Brothers Tried for Patricide."
13. Ibid., "Sons Statement Read to Jury."
14. *Philadelpahia Inquirer*, "Jury Is Selected in Father Slaying."
15. Ibid.
16. Stone, e-mail to the author.
17. Ibid.
18. Ibid.
19. *Philadelphia Evening Bulletin*, "Brothers Tried for Patricide."
20. Ibid., "Sons Statement Read to Jury."
21. *Philadelpahia Inquirer*, "Sons 'Figured' to Kill Father."
22. Ibid., "Brothers Win Point in Trial."
23. *Philadelphia Evening Bulletin*, "Sons Statement Read to Jury."
24. Ibid.
25. Ibid.
26. Ibid.
27. Ibid.
28. *Philadelpahia Inquirer*, "Brothers Admit Slaying, Tell of Beatings."
29. Ibid.
30. *Philadelphia Evening Bulletin*, "Sons Statement Read to Jury."
31. Ibid., "Brothers Acquitted."
32. Schlesinger, "Sexual Homicide."
33. *Philadelphia Evening Bulletin*, "State Asks Mercy in Father Killing."
34. Ibid.
35. Ibid.
36. Ibid.
37. *Philadelpahia Inquirer*, "Jury Holds Brothers' Fate in Killing."
38. Ibid.
39. *Philadelphia Evening Bulletin*, "State Asks Mercy in Father Killing."
40. *Philadelpahia Inquirer*, "Jury Holds Brothers' Fate in Killing."
41. Ibid.
42. *Philadelphia Evening Bulletin*, "Brothers Freed."

43. Ibid.
44. Ibid.
45. Ibid.
46. Ibid.

Chapter 8

47. *Chester Times*, "D'Amore Brothers to Share Equally in Dad's Estate."
48. Ibid.
49. Ibid.

Chapter 9

50. Smith, interview by author.
51. Meehan, "Jury Verdict Critized."
52. Wiley, "Free After 50 Days in Shadows."
53. Ibid.
54. Ibid.
55. Ibid.
56. Ibid.
57. Ibid.

WORKS CITED

Chester Times. "D'Amore Brothers to Share Equally in Dad's Estate." May 20, 1950.

Daubert v. Merrell Dow Pharmaceutical, Inc. 509 U.S. 579, 592 (1993).

Fahy, Michael. E-mail to the author, April 5, 2015.

Maier, Shana L. E-mail to the author, March 21, 2015.

May, Rollo. *The Meaning of Anxiety*. Toronto, CA: Ronald Press, 1950.

Meehan, John J. "Jury Verdict Critized." *Chester Times*, January 13, 1950.E

Parson v. State. 81 AL 557, 2 So 854, 865 (1886).

Philadelphia Evening Bulletin. "Brothers Acquitted." January 10, 1950.

———. "Brothers Freed." January 10, 1950.

———. "Brothers Tried for Patricide." January 4, 1950.

———. "Sons Statement Read to Jury." January 4, 1950.

———. "State Asks Mercy in Father Killing." January 9, 1950.

———. "Torture Blaimed on Slain Father." Januray 6, 1950.

Philadelpahia Inquirer. "Brothers Acquitted." January 10, 1950.

———. "Brothers Admit Slaying, Tell of Beatings." January 6, 1950.

———. "Brothers Win Point in Trial." January 5, 1950.

———. "Jurors Hold Fate of 2 in Father Killing." January 10, 1950.

———. "Jury Holds Brothers' Fate in Killing." January 10, 1950.

———. "Jury Is Selected in Father Slaying." January 4, 1950.

———. "Sons 'Figured' to Kill Father." January 5, 1950.

Pickrin, Wade E. *The Psychology Book: From Shamonism to Cutting-Edge Neuroscience, 250 Years in the History of Psychology*. New York: Sterling, 2014.

Schlesinger, Louis B. "Sexual Homicide: Differentiating Catathymic and Compulsive Murder." *Aggression and Violent Behavior* 1, no. 4 (2005): 242–56.

Smith, Jack. Interview by author. April 13, 2015.

Stone, Matthew C. E-mail to the author, April 7, 2015.

Wiley, Doris B. "Free After 50 Days in Shadows, D'Amores Hope for 'Normal Life.'" *Chester Times*, January 11, 1950.

INDEX

INDEX

ABOUT THE AUTHOR

Thomas George Deitman is a freelance author with an interest in criminal and legal matters. He has a law enforcement background and hold a bachelor's degree in paralegal studies with an emphasis on criminal law. This is his first book published by The History Press. Thomas lives with his wife, Olivia, in Parkside, Pennsylvania.